D1880793

# CAPITAL THEORY
# AND
# ECONOMIC ANALYSIS

# CAPITAL THEORY AND ECONOMIC ANALYSIS

Dr. KAMALA SUBRAMANIAM

**Gian Publishing House**

29/6 SHAKTI NAGAR • DELHI-110007 • INDIA

GIAN PUBLISHING HOUSE
29/6, Shakti Nagar, Delhi-110007

© 1987, KAMALA SUBRAMANIAM

ISBN 81-212-0089-X

PRINTED IN INDIA

---

Published by Mrs. Gayatri Garg for Gian Publishing House, Delhi and Printed at Mohan Printing Corpn., Delhi-110007.

# Preface

I HAD the good fortune to be a student of Prof. Gautam Mathur who is an inspiring teacher, it was not surprising, therefore, that I became deeply interested in the Theory of Capital. As a UGC Scholar I worked under his able guidance for my doctorate degree on Multiple Switching. His emphasis on economic logic and the use of mathematics as a tool has influenced me to a great extent.

I have relied on the Sraffa-Neumann Model developed by Prof. G. Mathur, for a frame of analysis. I have tried to acknowledge this, wherever possible. However, I may not have been completely successful in my attempt.

I have made an attempt to cover various aspects of the Theory of Capital from the classicals to post-Sraffians in this book. Starting from what is capital, I have tried to trace the history of basic concepts and important controversies in Capital Theory. I thought this would help the reader to get an insight into the evolution of the concepts which may in turn highlight the issues in the controversies. The capital theoretic base of classical, neo-classical and post-Keynesian Schools has been analysed with a view to understand the importance for Capital Theory in Economic Analysis. The limitations of the traditional approach to Multiple Switching is critically examined and an alternative approach is explored.

Prof. Ramakrishna, Director, Centre or Economic and Social Studies, Hyderabad, was kind enough to go through my first draft and offer his valuable comments. His suggestions were very helpful to me.

Dr. Ch. Raghuram, Professor of Economics, Osmania University, evinced keen interest in my work. His comments were valuable, especially suggestions on the draft of the last chapter helped me to make it more lucid.

In the formative stages of the work I had the benefit of discussing certain issues with Mr. W. Veerabhadra Rao, Reader in Economics, Osmania University.

I am also grateful to Mr. A. G. Moss, Research Associate, Department of Economics, Osmania University, who readily helped me to read the proofs.

Miss Prabha Pant, Lecturer in Economics, Department of Economics, helped me to organise the Bibliography in record time.

I thank Mr. M. Anand who typed several drafts with meticulous care, inspite of his heavy work load and Mr. A. Satya Reddy who has drawn the diagrams.

Finally, I would like to place on record the help I received from Prof. M. Naimuddin my husband who has been a most helpful critic, and frequent discussions with him has improved the clarity of my exposition.

In spite of all the valuable suggestions received, I must add, I am entirely responsible for the deficiencies that may have remained.

KAMALA SUBRAMANIAM

*Department of Economics*
*Osmania University*
*Hyderabad-500 007*

# Contents

CHAPTER I

# Introduction

DESCRIPTION of Capital is simple and unambiguous, therefore, there is in general, consensus about what capital is in economic theory. Production of goods involves composite inputs such as raw materials, wage goods to support labour during the process of production as well as physical capital goods that aid labour. In general capital includes all these components. Capital is, sub-classified into, working capital, consisting of raw material, wages and fixed capital. The former are used up during the process of production and the latter being durable last for more than one production period.

There is, therefore, no difficulty in enumerating the spectrum of capital goods in terms of plants, equipment of various types, tools and implements of different kinds. The difficulty arises in conceptualising capital so that its physical role in production is captured while its special characteristics are retained.

The concept of capital, has been a subject to change, like many other concepts, as economic theory evolved over time. Traditionally, three aspects of capital were emphasised, (a) capital is a produced means of production, produced for the specific purpose of aiding labour in the production of consumption goods ; (b) the use of capital in production involves sacrifice of time, and (c) diversion of resources from the production of consumption goods.

**Classical School**

For the classicals the only important primary factor of production is labour. The work of labour transforms the free gifts of nature into different forms of wealth. However, they were aware that the use of capital goods increased the productivity of labour, but as production of capital goods involves time, time through which labour must be supported. Capitalists require wage fund in order to command labour. The time factor in the production of capital goods was considered all important so that capital for the classicals is wage fund, necessary to advance to labour while they produced capital goods.

In economic literature it is stated very often[1] that in classical theory, capital is wage fund and capital goods were regarded as embodied wage fund of earlier periods.

However, in Ricardo's writings, when he generalises his corn model (which implies malleability of capital), capital is no longer circulating capital. In fact it is clear that capital goods are not regarded from the length-wise section as embodied labour, but capital includes fixed and working capital, entering various interlinked processes of production. His search for an invariant measure of value is itself, a result of being aware of the complications that arise in the theory of value as a result of introduction of fixed capital along with non-uniform composition of, fixed to circulating capital between a system of interlinked processes which produce a set of goods simultaneously.[2]

Ricardo, therefore, did not use the wages fund concept of capital in general, capital included not only raw materials and wages for labour, but machines as well, machines which are specific in form and function and belonged to different degree of durability.[3]

**Neo-classical School**

Following the general classical tradition Jevons views capital as an advance of subsistence to labour, but he emphasises the time dimension, the period over which this advance is made is also important. Capital according to him "Consists merely of the aggregate of those commodities which are required for sustaining labourers of any kind or class engaged in work".[4] Capital is a two dimensional concept for Jevons consisting of labour and time, it includes the amount of labour invested and the time over which it remains invested (period of production). The product of these two elements is the concept of capital used by Jevons, which he calls 'amount of investment'. For example, 5 units of labour invested for one year or one unit of labour invested for five years would both be 5 units of capital invested, in Jevons' analysis.

Although the time element is given prominence by Jevons, heterogenity of inputs is ignored. For he uses money prices of inputs to arrive at the aggregate inputs glossing over the difficulties that arise in the solution of relative shadow prices which in turn depends on the distribution of income. Thus, Jevons even by using a simple concept of capital—working capital, does not deal with heterogenity of inputs successfully.

**Bohm Bawerk**

The Austrian capital theorists start their analysis of capital by ranking goods in accordance with the stage to which they belong in the production process. At one extreme, are the original or natural resources ranked as goods of the highest order, while at the other end are the goods for final consumption, ranked as first order goods. In between are the capital goods called intermediate goods, ranked further according to their stage of intermediation. In the Austrian school, greater number of intermediate goods would imply greater degree of roundaboutness of production.

While ranking goods according to the stage of production is a common feature, it must be noted that the peculiarity of the Austrian school lies in the fact that the different stages of production exist at different times, so that in their system, greater intermediation (roundaboutness) would mean greater time lag of production.

Like the classicals Bohm Bawerk regarded labour and nature as the two original productive powers and did not accept capital as a factor of production.

Although capital was not a factor of production on par with land and labour, the sacrifice of time involved in increasing the degree of roundaboutness was considered worthwhile since, roundabout methods were said to be more fruitful.[5]

The concept of capital used by Bohm Bawerk for analytical purposes in general, is circulating capital, capital goods were regarded by him as stored up labour and land of an earlier period.

Although 'Capital' is circulating capital in his analysis, his arguments are based on examples drawn from the actual world, where productivity is increased when bare-hand process is replaced by a simple capital good, like for example fishing net made by a fisherman by taking time off from fishing with bare-hands, which when complete, helps him to catch more fish than he did with his bare hands.

However, capital goods which made labour more productive, had to be traced backwards in time to arrive at their cost in order to arrive at the value of inputs at any stage of production in time.

Tracing a good's inputs over time, over the various layers of production deemed to exist over time, will no doubt, lead to a measure of its historic cost, which would reflect the conditions of production which existed when its production originated. But historic cost will in no way be related, in general, to the conditions of production, where the fixed capital good enters the interlinked system of processes, along with other inputs to produce a set of goods simultaneously in Unit time.

**Knut Wicksell**

Wicksell defines capital as "The term......includes all auxiliaries to production, with the exception of natural forces in their original form and direct human labour".[6] His definition of capital includes plants where production of goods take place, tools and implements that aid labour, raw materials and wages advance to labour. Capital defined thus, is capable of two different interpretations, it can be either regarded from the cross section point of view where capital goods are a vector of investment goods that enter various processes of production co-existing in time, or from the length-wise section as saved up labour and land of an earlier period. Wicksell like Bohm Bawerk, chose to view capital from the length-wise section, as saved up land and labour of an earlier period.

**J.B. Clark**

Clark starts his analysis on capital by making a clear distinction between capital as a fund and capital goods. He deviates sharply from both the classical and Austrian school by regarding capital, distinct from capital goods, as a factor of production. For J.B. Clark, capital is a "Permanent Fund of productive wealth, and is what is commonly meant by 'money' invested in productive goods, the identity of which is forever changing".[7]

Thus, for Clark, Capital, a Fund is a factor of production, is productive and earns a return.

The physical counterpart of this Fund, capital goods, Clark admits are specific in design and function in the short run. He nevertheless assumes that capital goods are malleable and tries to justify the assumption on the ground, that accumulation in the long run is accompanied by changes in capital structure.

**Joan Robinson**

Joan Robinson stresses the need to make a clear distinction between 'Capital' which is physical, a means of production with specific characteristics of technical nature and 'Capital' in the sense of command over finance. Further, she highlights the importance of heterogeneity of capital goods, specificness of design and the nature of man to machine ratio as the relevant features that need to be taken care of conceptualising capital for analytical purposes. Her attack on Neo-classical capital theory centres round the invalidity of the assumption of malleability of capital or the use of prices to convert the set of heterogeneous inputs to a homogeneous unit, ignoring the fact that relative prices and distributions are mutually dependant.

Her stand on the nature of capital is clear for she writes "the list of goods is quite specific. It is so many particular objects called blast furnaces, overcoats etc., etc. Goods grouped under the same name differ from each other in details of their physical specification and these must not be over looked. Differences in their ages are also important."[8]

It must be noted that the stimulus for recent debates on measurement of capital was provided by her article,[9] where she questions the concept of aggregate capital used as a factor of production in Neo-Classical production functions.

Joan Robinson uses one capital good model or two goods model for analysis. The model with one capital good discards the assumption of malleability of capital implicit in the one good model of the traditional type where corn is the only good produced, it represents both the consumption good and capital good (seed). In contrast, the two goods model reflects roundaboutness of production through the introduction of the concept of capital good which is used in both processes of production to aid labour to produce goods.[10]

**Swan**

As a reaction to Joan Robinson's attack on Neo-Classical concept of capital, Swan came up with a growth model using the analogy of Meccano sets, to ward off "the index number, birds and Joan Robinson herself".[11] Capital in his model "is made up of large number of identical Meccano sets which never wear out and can be put together, taken apart and reassembled with negligible cost or decay."[12] Capital can be made to work with various proportions of land and labour, to produce different composition of outputs. Further, Capital absorbs technical progress without time lag or cost. When the Meccano set is reassembled, it can be made to reflect technical progress.

Thus, assuming capital (Meccano sets) to be ever lasting on the one hand and completely malleable on the other, Swan makes an attempt to arrive at a value concept of capital independent of distribution. The concept of capital analogous to Meccano sets is used to over come the difficulties that arise in conceptualising heterogeneous, durable capital goods which have a time dimension which makes aggregation more complicated than the aggregation of heterogeneous goods at a point of time as in cross sectional analysis. The durability assumption leads to joint products, which complicates the process of aggregation further, the Meccano set concept of capital helps to overcome the problem of joint production as well.

**P. Samuelson**

Among the Neo-Classicals, mention must be made of Samuelson

as he has attempted to rescue the Jelly Capital concept of J.B. Clark with his Surrogate Production Function.[13]

He starts his analysis with an admission that capital theory can be developed on the basis of complete set of heterogeneous physical goods, avoiding the use of Jelly capital. However, he claims that it is possible in some cases to predict how a heterogeneous capital goods model would behave, with the help of a Jelly Capital Model.

In his model each capital good has a specific use and when combined with a fixed capital good produces either itself or a homogeneous consumption good. Further, in his model, one capital good cannot be converted into another, the structure of capital goods can only change with time, skill and real resources. Thus, the concept of capital used in his model resembles closely capital goods used in production in an actual economy. The heterogenity of capital goods however, turns out to be deceptive. For, by making a suitable assumption, Samuelson converts his general heterogeneous durable capital model to a very special case. He assumes that the proportion of inputs in the process which produces the consumption good to be the same as in the process that produces the capital good. This assumption makes the relative prices independant of distribution.

The surrogate production function resembles the Jelly capital model only due to this simplifying assumption made as regards the input composition between the processes of a technique.

Samuelson's model is a case where a model is built which apprarently resembles the characteristics of production in the real world, but which is converted into an over simplified model with the help of suitable assumptions.

**Von-Neumann Model**

In Von-Neumann Model[14] the concept and description of capital coincide. For, in Neumann model, goods produce goods, every good is said to enter the production of every other, directly or indirectly, hence at a moment of time all goods form stocks and are capital. Although goods (stocks) can be classified into consumption goods, raw material and fixed capital equipment, in conformity with conventional usage, capital goods do not belong to a special category in Von-Neumann model. Since capital goods are viewed from the cross-section point of view, as goods entering the interlinked system of processes, where the system as a whole with the help of goods as inputs produce more goods as outputs, the concept of capital good as an intermediate good is blurred. For there is no time lag involved, in the sense that the production of consumption good is suspended while the capital good is made, which when complete, aids the production of a greater quantum of consumption goods.

In this system of interlinked processes, both capital goods conventionally called intermediate goods and final goods are produced simultaneously. The traditional view of capital as a link between the present stage and final stage of consumption good production over time is no longer valid.

In this model, when the goods enters the process of production as an input, if it is a raw material or a wage good consumed by workers during the process of production, it gets a zero entry on the output side. In case the good is a durable capital equipment, the entry on the output side would be non-zero, for fixed capital is depicted as a joint product of the processes of production. Von-Neumann assumes indefinite life of capital goods. Thus, heterogenity of inputs in general and of capital goods in particular is reflected fully in Neumann's concept of capital. Further, the model can be made to take care of any degree of disaggregation, for it is possible to analytically treat. different types of ploughs as different capital goods. In fact the level of aggregation is left to the discretion of the analyst as it depends on the nature of the problem under study. In Von-Neumann model, therefore, characteristics of physical capital goods can be fully represented, characteristics of specificness of design, function and durability. Thus, the cenceptualisation of capital retains the essential characteristics of the description of capital.

**P. Sraffa**

Sraffa starts his analysis[15] with a very simple model where processes of production depict commodities producing commodities without the aid of machines. The system of processes together, produce just enough to replace inputs, which consists of means of production and sustenance for workers. A system of relative prices emerge from the technical conditions of production which when used, helps to bring about the original distribution of inputs between processes. Sraffa, with the help of this simple model proves that the system can exist period after period over time. In this model the concept of capital used is working capital.

Next Sraffa introduces production with a surplus,[16] with uniform wage rate and rate of profit. He also assumes that wages are paid post factum. In this case he shows that the distribution of surplus must be in proportion to the means of production of inputs. Since the inputs are heterogeneous in his model, though there are no machines, prices have still to be determined to aggregate, the inputs. But prices are not independant of rate of profit, hence Sraffa demonstrates the need for simultaneous determination of relative prices and the rate of profit. In this case the concept of capital used by Sraffa is raw material inputs, since wage is paid post factum, and machines are not used in production. However, the process of production is considered as an interlinked system, so that capital is regarded from the cross-section point of view, as a set of goods entering the processes of production as inputs at a moment of time, which produce a set of goods as outputs. Since machines are absent, there is however, no joint production in his simple model.

In Parts II and III of his book[17] Sraffa generalises his simple models to include capital goods in the process of production. Like in Von-Neumann model, in the fixed capital good model of Sraffa, capital goods are treated as joint products. But Sraffa brings his model closer to real world situations by dropping the assumption of everlasting equipment made by Von-Neumann. In Sraffa system a fixed capital good entering the process of production is depicted as capital good on the output side, as a year older than it was in the means of production.

Thus, in Sraffa's system there will be as many unknowns (prices) as the economic life of a fixed capital good. For capital goods of different ages are treated as distinct goods and their prices emerge as different, when the system of equations derived from the processes is solved for prices.

The concept of capital used b Sraffa reflects its description closely for, it not only reflects heterogenity specificness of form, function and durability, it also allows difference in age of similar machines to get reflected in its prices. Sraffa, however, assumes 'one hosse shay'.

## II

Theory of capital forms the basis for some important aspects of economic theory. Its relevance is obviously apparent in the field of choice of techniques and the theory of distribution. The classicals were primarily concerned with the dynamic process of accumulation of stock.[18] Their analysis of profits on accumulated capital was in the nature of identifying its role in the process of accumulation. Theory of value, analysed with care and considerable insight by David Ricardo, was in the context of accumulation. To the Classicals capital theory was not merely the theory of value, but included the origin of capital and the process of the growth of capital stock.

In the Bohm-Bawerkian System, a greater degree or roundaboutness implied accumulation of capital, which in turn can only be achieved through the introduction of greater degree of roundaboutness. Bohm-Bawerk in search of an optimum degree of roundaboutness was given the labour force and the wage fund, which would in turn lead to an optimum degree of accumulation. In this context he wanted a measure of the degree of roundaboutness, which reflects not only total labour input, but its distribution over time as well. Thus, the origin of capital and the process of its accumulation were the important issues in Bohm-Bawerk's capital theory, a value theory was evolved, only to capture suitably the relevant aspect of accumulation.

Knut Wicksell considered a process of accumulation with capital deepening, over time. In this context he found a measure of capital in terms of an average period of production unsatisfactory, since valuation through the average production period is not independant of the rate of profit.

Capital theorists both classical and neo-classical thus, analysed the origin of capital and the relationship between the rate of profit and accumulation. Their interest in the measurement of capital in value terms, was the natural outcome of their primary concern to study the forces that contribute to the accumulation of stock.

Growth theory gained importance after 1940, with it, the closely related problem of distribution received attention. The theory of value which is indispensable in analysing distribution of income naturally came to the forefront. The importance of capital theory came to be recognised when choice of techniques and distribution were analysed in the context of growth.

However, the controversy in capital theory in recent debates has been on the measurement of capital in value terms. The modern debates in the theory of capital do not deal with explanations to how profit originates or with the forces that induce accumulation, this aspect of capital theory came to be dealt with by the theory of economic growth, the debates emphasise the value aspect of capital theory.

The attempt to develop growth theory, independent of the theory of capital raises some basic issues. As growth models deal with the process of accumulation, they must be based on some concept of capital. Further, as growth overtime depends on the distribution of the surplus of an economy, closely related issues of distribution theory have to be necessarily analysed in the theory of growth. The theory of distribution is complicated, in general, due to heterogeneity of inputs and outputs and durable nature of physical goods which exist in the real world production. For the measure of the surplus and its distribution in proportion to the heterogeneous inputs of different processes of production, calls for the simultaneous determination of relative prices and the rate of profit, the given wage rate.

Thus, the existence of heterogeneity of inputs and outputs along with the surplus of the system, theory of value and distribution become mutually dependant, a simultaneous determination of relative prices and rate of profit becomes inevitable.[19] Further, as a growth model cannot be formulated without a concept of capital, the value theory that underlies a growth model emerges from the concept of capital that forms the basis of a growth model. If, for example, the growth model assumes a single good which plays the dual role of the consumption good as well as capital good, the theory of value becomes redundant, if the growth model allows heterogeneity of inputs but assumes malleability of capital the theory of value gets relegated to the background. On the other hand, if the growth model is based on assumption of heterogeneity in inputs/outputs along with capital goods as being specific in design and function, the theory of value becomes necessary though complex in nature.

In planned economic development, the problem of choice of techniques is tackled through the insight gained from the theory of capital.

One of the analytical tools developed to deal with the choice of techniques in theory of capital is the concept of production function. There are many forms of production functions in use, for, in general a production function is defined as a technical or engineering relation between input and output.[20]

As mentioned earlier, the neo-classical production function was questioned by Joan Robinson in her famous article 'The Production Function and Theory of Capital',[21] which led to a debate on the validity of aggregating heterogeneous capital so that capital can be regarded as a factor of production more or less on par with labour and land.

After the publication of Sraffa's book[22] in which he conclusively proves that there can be no aggregate concept of capital independent of distribution, the neo-classical types of production function where capital is factor of production are logically unacceptable.

However, production functions, which do not use the aggregate concept of capital have also been developed.[23] For this purpose, a technique is viewed as a set of interdependent processes with heterogeneous inputs and outputs. Where capital goods are inputs and are joint products of the system. Given the wage rate or rate of profit, the system of equations derived from the technique of production can be solved for relative prices, by imposing the condition of uniform rate of profit in all the used processes. The capital goods thus shadow priced along with other goods in the system, are given the distribution of income. The value of K/L thus obtained, and O/L for each technique are represented on the cartesian plane to get a scatter. The outer envelope forms the set of mutually non-superior techniques called the production function if the distribution changes the value of capital changes, in general, so that the production function has to be re-drawn.[24]

The relative prices of goods within a technique, including the price of the capital, goods are governed by the real wage rate, the rate of profit and the technological co-efficients of production, in this system. By assuming a uniform wage rate in all the processes of production, the role of productivities given by technology, in determining relative prices is brought out by G. Mathur. Techniques have been classified into three basic categories, in terms of their Wicksell Structure.[25]

The possibility of a technique termed as inferior at a wage rate joining the set of mutually non-superior techniques at a higher wage rate, emerging as a dominating technique at still higher wage rates is also examined by Mathur.[26]

A technique, emerging as the most profitable at two different wage rates being unprofitable in ranges in between was theoretically worked out by Sraffa,[27] leading to reswitching of techniques.

Thus, if capital is heterogeneous, its value (relative prices) is not independent of the wage rate (or rate of profit) even when the technique of production is constant. Therefore, when distribution changes, relative prices change, so that the set of eligible techniques are of changing composition. Theory of capital helps to keep constant track of the set of viable techniques in order that the optimum combination of techniques may be chosen on the path of development. A path of transition which takes a few decades of capital accumulation accompanied with structural change and change in distribution.

## REFERENCES

1. M. Dobb : *Theories of Value and Distribution since Adam Smith*, (CUP—Vikas Students' Edition, 1979) p. 42.

2. P. Sraffa (Ed) : *The Works and Correspondence of David Ricardo,* (Vol. I, Cambridge University Press, 1953), p. 30.
3. *Ibid.*
4. Jevons : *Theory of Political Economy* (London 1911, 4th Edition) p. 223.
5. M. Blaug : *Economic Theory in Retrospect*, (Cambridge University Press, 1978) p. 525.
6. K. Wicksell : *Lectures on Political Economy,* (Routledge & Kegan Paul, Vol. 1, 1934) pp. 144-145.
7. J.B. Clark : *The Distribution of Wealth* (Macmillan 1927), p. 157.
8. J. Robinson : "The Production Function and the Theory of Capital" in *Collected Economic Papers*, (Vol. 2, Blackwell, 1965) pp. 114-31—First Published in *Review of Economic Studies*, (Vol. 21, 1953-54), pp. 81-106.
9. *Ibid.*
10. J. Robinson : *The Accumulation of Capital,* (Macmillan, 1969) p. 75.
11. T.W. Swan : "Notes on Capital", *Capital and Growth*, Ed. G.C. Harcourt and N.F. Laing, (Penguin 1971) pp. 101-124, Excerpt from T.W. Swan, 'Economic Growth and Capital Accumulation', *Economic Record*, (Vol. 23, 1956), pp. 343-61.
12. *Ibid.*
13. P.A. Samuelson : "Parable and Realism in Capital Theory : The Surrogate Production Function", *Review of Economic Studies*, Vol. 39, 1962, pp. 193-206.
14. J. Von Neumann : 'A Model of General Economic Equilibrium', *Readings in the Theory of Growth.* A Selection of Papers from the *Review of Economic Studies*, Ed. by F.H. Hahn (Macmillan 1971) pp. 1-9.
15. P. Sraffa : *Production of Commodities by Means of Commodities,* (Cambridge University Press, 1973) pp. 3-5.
16. *Ibid.*, Chapter II.
17. *Ibid.*
18. J. Robinson and J. Eatwell : *An Introduction to Modern Economics,* (Tata McGraw Hill 1974), p. 15 .
19. P. Sraffa : *Production of Commodities by Means of Commidities,* (Cambridge University Press, 1973), p. 6.
20. L.R. Klein : *An Introduction to Econometrics* (Prentice Hall of India Ltd., New Delhi, 1965), p. 84.
21. J. Robinson : "The Production Function and the Theory of Capital", *Review of Economic Studies,* 1953, No. 21, pp. 81-106.

22. P. Sraffa : *Production of Commodities by Means of Commodities*, (Cambridge University Press, 1960).

23. G. Mathur : *Planning for Steady Growth*, (Basil, Blackwell, 1965), pp. 137-152.

24. *Ibid.*, pp. 167-177.

25. *Ibid.*, pp. 158-162.

26. *Ibid.*, pp. 184-187.

27. P. Sraffa : *Produciion of Commodities by Means of Commodities*, (Cambridge University Press, 1973), pp. 81-82.

CHAPTER II

# The Classical School and the Theory of Capital

### The Classicals

ADAM SMITH, David Ricardo, Thomas Robert Malthus, Nassau William Senior, John Stuart Mill, and Jean Baptiste say are regarded as important contributors to the Classical School. Among these leading classical economists, the analytical insight shown by Adam Smith and Ricardo in analysing the theory of value is significant.

### Adam Smith

Adam Smith starts his analysis of the determinants of relative values of commodities under the assumption of free land and unaided labour. Citing the analogy of hunting, he concludes that if a hunter takes twice as much time to kill a beaver than a deer, two deers will exchange for a beaver. Thus, in an economy which is in a primitive stage, relative values of goods would be governed by labour expended. However, in an economy which is no longer in a primitive stage, where capital aids labour, Adam Smith abandon's the labour theory of value. In the case of more than one factor of production used for making a good, Adam Smith states that the value of the commodity or its "natural price" is determined by the sum of, costs of production, which includes the payments made in terms of money to the factors of production such as wages, rents and profits. Thus, Adam Smith attempts to solve the problem of determination of relative values through the cost of production. However, this approach begs the question as to how, the factors of production themselves are priced ? For which no consistent answer is found in the analysis of wages, rents and profits in the works of Adam Smith.[1]

*David Ricardo* : Ricardo, in his search for the laws that govern distribution found that the theory of distribution is inseparably intertwined with the theory of value. In the calculation of the rate of surplus and rate of profit a theory of value becomes imperative. For, in order to arrive at these ratios, a set of heterogeneous goods which, generally, constitute the net product of the system and the means of production have to be made homogeneous by the use of relative prices or exchange values.

The calculation of the rate of profit is not complicated in the simple one good model that Ricardo developed to analyse the factors that govern distribution. In this model corn is the only good produced (output), while the inputs are, seed and advance of wages to labour (corn). Thus, the input, output and the surplus consist of the same good corn, so that the rate of profit on capital is the ratio of corn profit to the stock of corn, derived in physical units independent of any value theory. The one good model is an analytical device which brings the real factors to the forefront which contribute to the emergence of surplus, such as the real wage rate and the fertility of the soil. It established the inverse relationship of the wage rate and the rate of profit, given the technical conditions of production. Further, the one good model avoids the circularity that creeps in, the moment prices become necessary to convert a set heterogeneous goods to a common unit, circularity brought in by the interdependence of relative prices and the rate of profit.

In the Ricardian system profits are a residue, its existence is dependent on the availability of a surplus over wage costs on the marginal or no rent land. As accumulation and growth of population make extensive cultivation inevitable, the surplus, net of wage costs shrinks as less fertile land is brought under cultivation, which acts as a constraint on accumulation, ultimately ushering in the stationary state, in the absence of technical progress.

The classical distribution theory has been explained with the help of a diagram by W.J. Banmol.[2] The diagram is reproduced, since, the dynamics of the classical system, can be easily understood with its help.

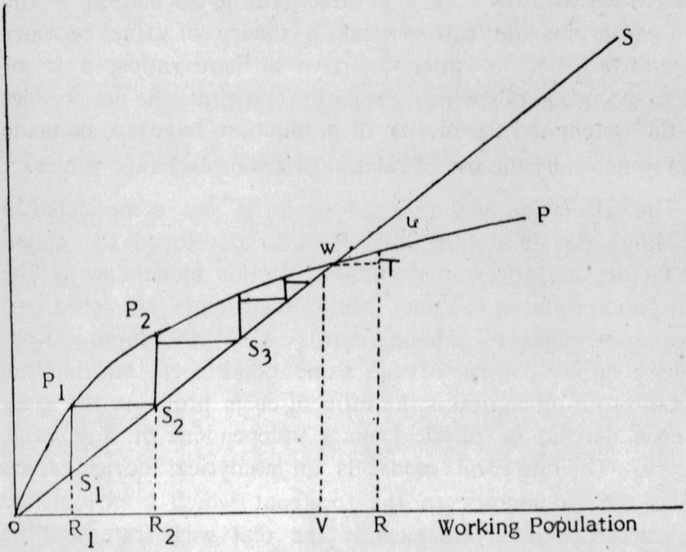


Diagram I

On the X-axis, the working population is measured, while on the Y-axis total wage and total product net of rent are measured. As total wage by working population would give the wage rate, the slope of the line OS passing through the origin gives the wage rate. The total product curve OP is drawn convex from above, reflecting the assumption of the law of diminishing returns and the assumption of increasing rent payments with the growth of population. In the diagram when population is $DR_1$ total product net of rent is $R_1 P_1$ at a range where population is greater, an equal increase in population *i.e.* $OR_1 = VR$ leads only to a small increase in total product TU. Initially, wages are at subsistence. Profits net of wages bill and rent will be positive. This induces further accumulation which will in turn increase wages to $R_1 P_1$, high wages in turn leads to increase in population, wage is reduced to subsistence once again, and profits emerge depicted by $S_2 P_2$ in the diagram, the existence of profits leads to accumulation which drives up wages, to further growth in population in response to higher wage rate ($OR_2$) followed by reduction of wage to subsistence leading to emergence of profits. This process continues till the straight line OS cuts the total product curve at W. Once the point W is reached, profits are zero, for at W total wages is equal to total product net of rent, even if wage rate is at subsistence. As the profits at W are zero, accumulation ceases, the economy sinks into stationary state with population stationary at OV. Profits, a residue in the Ricardian System is also a vehicle of accumulation, for the profits on stock accrue to the owners of stock, the capitalists, who invest a major share of it and thus bring about further accumulation.

In this background Ricardo was soon made aware[3] of the limitations of the one good model, since even if corn was the only good produced, wage earners will not be satisfied with corn, and would need other manufactured goods and therefore heterogeneity of inputs and outputs cannot be avoided.

It is in this context, while the dynamic process of accumulation was analytically examined along with the theory of distribution, Ricardo felt the need to develop another branch of capital theory—the theory of value—on lines compatible with an unambiguous measure of distribution of a given volume of output. He began his search for an "invariant measure of value" which could be used to convert the heterogeneous inputs and outputs of production process to a common unit, which would itself remain "invariant" to changes in distribution. He was, in other words, looking for a set of relative prices independent of the rate of profit.

The link between the relative prices and the rate of profit which leads to circular reasoning, cannot be avoided by the use of market prices to aggregate the inputs in the process of production of a good for the input prices include the profits of the capitalists who produced them, using a different set of processes. For example consider a simple model where labour and equipment e, together produce the C-good C. To arrive at the rate of profit in the production of C, the inputs of the process, namely wage paid to the worker W in terms of C and the equipment $e_1$ will have to be aggregated. If market prices are used to aggregate the inputs, say $P_0$ and $P_1$ respectively, the following value equation is obtained, where R is the coefficient of profit $(P_0W+e_1P_1) = CP_0$ ...... (1)

$$\therefore R - \frac{CP_0}{P_0W+e_1P_1}$$

However, R obtained through equation (1) is not independent of the rate of profit, for the price of equipment $e_1$ made in another process includes the rate of profit. If it is assumed for simplicity that labour and $e_1$ make $e_1$, we get the corresponding value equation from the $e_1$ making Process,

$$(WP_0+e_1P_1)R = e_1P_1 \qquad \text{...... (2)}$$

From equation (2) it is clear that $P_1$, the price of equipment $e_1$, is not independent of the rate of profit. Thus, while the input prices are dependant on the rate of profit, the total value of inputs found by using market prices is needed to calculate the rate of profit for the process in which they enter as inputs in production to make the good in question. Ricardo was well aware of this interdependence of processes, an interdependence which affects the relative prices of commodities.

In the early stages of his analysis on theory of value, Ricardo was convinced that the basis of exchange value of commodities is the labour embodied.[4] Unlike Adam Smith who felt that the labour theory of value was valid only in a society which is yet to accumulate capital Ricardo argued that even when capital goods aided labour, the labour theory of value would hold subject only to minor modification—"The exchangeable value of the commodities produced would be in proportion to the labour bestowed on their production ; not on their immediate production only, but on all those implements or machines required to give effect to the particular labour to which they were applied".[5]

However, Ricardo who looked at production as a system of interlinked processes soon discovered the limitations of the labour theory of value as an invariant measure. For the labour theory of value, if it is to be invariant to distribution, demands a proportionality between relative prices (exchange value) and quantity of labour bestowed, a proportionality which disappears when the composition of inputs between processes is different. For, when the value of fixed capital to wage ratio (K/LW) differs between processes, a difference in distribution, say a higher wage rate (or lower rate of profit) affects different processes in different proportions. If uniform rate of profit is to prevail in all the processes of the interlinked system it calls for an adjustment of relative prices, thus, the emergence of a new set of relative values is imperative, although no change has taken place in the technique of production, and hence there has been no change in labour requirements. For example, consider an interlinked system* of process where three goods are produced where all the three goods enter directly or indirectly in the production of these goods. If the goods produced are consumption good C, the equipment $e_1$ required as input to aid labour in the C-good process and equipment $e_2$ which produces the second order capital good $e_1$, with the help of labour and $e_2$, the highest order capital which reproduces itself with the aid of labour. The set of processes, called a technique[6] is represented, as follows, where wage is paid in advance of production in terms of the consumption good C, and $e_1$ and $e_2$ are assumed durable.

---

* Ricardo argued that the difference in the ratio of circulating to fixed capital between processess is the basic cause of change in relative prices with change in distribution even when the method of production is constant. But his examples are defective as the inputs are in money prices perhaps due to the solution of simultaneous equations not being known in his times. The Sraffa-Neumann model is chosen here, as it brings to the forefront the logic that Ricardo tried to explain.

TECHNIQUE A

| Men | C | $e_1$ | $e_2$ | | C | $e_1$ | $e_2$ |
|---|---|---|---|---|---|---|---|
| 1 | 1 | 1 | 0 | ⟶ | 10 | 1 | 0 |
| 1 | 1 | 0 | 1 | ⟶ | 0 | 6 | 1 |
| 1 | 1 | 0 | 1 | ⟶ | 0 | 0 | 1+1 |

The value equations derived from the set of processes are

$(1+P_1)\ R = 10+P_1$ ...... (1)

$(1+P_2)\ R = 6P_1+P_2$ ...... (2)

$(1+P_2)\ R = 2P_2$ ...... (3)

Where, the relative prices are $1 : P_1 : P_2$, where the consumption good is the numeraire of the system, and R the coefficient of profit.

When these equations are solved for prices, we get 1 : 8.3659 : 50.1955.

For the same set of processes, if wage rate is taken higher (2) the same technique of production is depicted as follows :

TECHNIQUE A

| Men | C | $e_1$ | $e_2$ | | C | $e_1$ | $e_2$ |
|---|---|---|---|---|---|---|---|
| 1 | 2 | 1 | 0 | ⟶ | 10 | 1 | 0 |
| 1 | 2 | 0 | 1 | ⟶ | 0 | 6 | 1 |
| 1 | 2 | 0 | 1 | ⟶ | 0 | 0 | 1+1 |

The corresponding value equations are :

$(2+P_1)\ R = 10+P_1$ ...... (1)

$(2+P_2)\ R = 6P_1+P_2$ ...... (2)

$(2+P_2)\ R = 2P_2$ ...... (3)

Solving for relative prices we obtain :

$$1 : P_1 : P_2 = 1 : 6.821952 : 40.931712$$

The uniform rate of profit is 90 per cent for this technology with wage rate being 2 bags of corn.

Thus, for the same technique of production, and therefore same labour requirements, two sets of relative prices are obtained when distribution changes.

In this case, when K/LW is different in different processes of production of a good, expressing relative prices of goods in terms of one of the goods as numeraire does not lead to an unambiguous measure of changes in relative values, due to changes in distribution, for, the price of the numeraire commodity itself is subject to change when distribution changes. A given difference in wage rate (or r), affects the K/LW ratio of all processes including the process of production of the numeraire commodity, in different proportions. Hence, an observed difference in price of commodity A (Say) in terms of the numeraire could be partly due to a change in the price of the commodity 'A' and partly due to a change in the numeraire commodity itself whose value also gets adjusted in order that the same rate of profit may be obtained in all the processes. Ricardo was well aware of the non-proportionality between relative values and quantity of labour when the value of equipment per man to wage ratio happens to be different processes or when machines used, are not equally durable. In such cases he remarks, "with every rise of wages, in proportion as the capital employed in any occupation consists of circulating capital, its produce will be of greater relative value than the goods produced in another occupation where a less proportion of circulating and a greater proportion of fixed capital are employed."[7]

Thus, the limitations of the labour theory of value as invariant to distribution was brought out by Ricardo. However, he was not successful in the task he set himself—the task of finding a measure of value invariant to distribution, a measure on par with standard measures of the physical world.

## REFERENCES

1. M. Blaug, *Economic Theory in Retrospect* (Cambridge University Press, 1978) pp. 40-41,

2. W.J. Baumol, *Economic Dynamics, An Introduction*, (Macmillan, 1963), pp. 18-21.
3. J. Robinson and J. Eatwell, *An Introduction to Modern Economics*, (Tata McGraw Hill, 1974), p. 19.
4. P. Sraffa (Ed.), *The Works and Correspondence of David Ricardo*, (Cambridge University Press, Vol. II, 1966), pp. 34-35.
5. P. Sraffa (Ed.), *The Works and Correspondence of David Ricardo*, (Cambridge University Press, Vol. I, 1953), p. 24.
6. G. Mathur, *Planning for Steady Growth*, (Basil Blackwell, 1966), p. 45.
7. P. Sraffa (Ed.), *The Works and Correspondence of David Ricardo*, (Cambridge University Press, Vol. I, 1953), p. 58.

## CHAPTER III

# The Neo-Classical School and the Theory of Capital*

### The Austrian School

THE AUSTRIAN School consists of the founder, Carl Menger (1840-1921) and two of his disciples Friederich Von Wieser (1851-1926) and Eugen Von Bohm-Bawerk (1851-1913). Carl Menger and Von Wieser were mainly concerned with the theory of value, Menger was the first to clearly enunciate the equi-

---

Note : * Theory derived from the Works of first and second generation marginalists, is generally known as neo-classical theory. The neo-classicals whose works are taken up for detailed analysis in this Chapter are Walras, Wicksell and J.B. Clark, as the works of these are germane to the issues discussed in this Chapter. Among, the neo-classicals, Samuelson's Surrogate Production Function is discussed in the Introduction, while Swan's concept of Capital is analysed in this Chapter. Thus, the author-wise analysis of the works in the neo-classical School is on a selective basis—selected on the basis of the relevance of their Contributions to the issues discussed. However, the main propositions of the neo-classical school as a whole pertaining to Capital Theory are also critically examined in summary form in this chapter. See G.C. Harcourt, *Some Cambridge Controversies in the Theory of Capital*, (CUP 1972), p. 2. Also see Joan Robinson and Eatwell, *An Introduction in Modern Economics* (TMH Edition, McGraw Hill, 1974, p. 34.

marginal principle, while Von Wieser coined the term "marginal utility".[1]

The third important member of the Austrian School, Bohm-Bawerk showed interest in the Theory of Capital, his contributions to the theory of capital is recognised as significant.

*Bohm Bawerk* : The Austrian School viewed capital from the lengthwise section based on their observation of capitalistic production in its early stage of development, i.e., they regarded different stages of production to exist over time. Natural resources were considered as highest order goods, while the final consumption goods were ranked as the first order goods. The conversion of natural resources to consumption goods involved different stages, greater the number of stages greater would be the number of capital goods, intermediate goods, ranked further according to their stage of intermediation.

The use of capital goods is a roundabout means of converting natural resources to C-goods and since in their system, the different intermediate stages of production are not said to co-exist in time, the use of intermediate goods leads to a longer period of production or roundaboutness ; which in turn implies greater time lag in the conversion of natural resources to final consumption goods.

The difference between the lengthwise section approach to capital which was the Austrian approach to capital and the cross section approach to capital found in the works of Von-Neumann, P. Sraffa and G. Mathur is best explained with an example.

*Lengthwise Section Approach to Capital* : Consider a fisherman in an economy which is in pre-capitalistic stage. The fisherman has been fishing without a net, fishing with his bare hands. If he decides to produce a net one fine day, the Austrian Capital Theorists approach to capital would lead to the conceptualisation of the process of production of the net as follows. The fisherman who has taken the decision to produce a net would divert all his working hours to its production and live on wild fruit or alternatively he, would divert a major part of his time to the making of a net and the rest of the time he would continue to fish with bare hands to catch enough fish to sustain himself.

Now suppose he works 5 hours per day on making the net. Further, to make the net three different stages of production are needed, the Cotton has to be gathered, cotton spun into yarn and the yarn made into a net. Each of these stages can be represented by a process as follows. If the fisherman can gather 2.5 kgs of cotton in one day (five hours) the process could be depicted as,

| Man-day | | Cotton | |
|---|---|---|---|
| 1 | ⟶ | 2.5 | (1) |

If the fisherman can make 5 meters of yarn with 2.5 kgs of cotton in one day, the second process can be depicted as,

| Man-day | | Cotton | | Yarn | |
|---|---|---|---|---|---|
| 1 | ⟶ | 2.5 | ⟶ | 5 | (2) |

Finally, if the fisherman can make .1 square meter of the net with 5 meters of yarn, process (3) could be depicted as

| Man-day | | Yarn | | Net |
|---|---|---|---|---|
| 1 | ⟶ | 5 | ⟶ | .1 |

All the three processes needed to make the net could be depicted as a set of processes as below, in matrix A.

**MATRIX A**

| Man-day | Cotton | Yarn | Net | | Cotton | Yarn | Net |
|---|---|---|---|---|---|---|---|
| 1 | 0 | 0 | 0 | → | 2.5 | 0 | 0 |
| 1 | 2.5 | 0 | 0 | → | 0 | 5 | 0 |
| 1 | 0 | 5 | 0 | → | 0 | 0 | .1 |

In the lengthwise section approach to capital, the three processes of production do not co-exist in time, that is, each process is a stage of production which is sequentially brought into existence over time. If the matrix A is the technical datum, then the fisherman would spend the first 10 days in collecting cotton for he requires 25 kgs of cotton to make enough yarn with which he could complete the net. Next the fisherman is visualised to spend 10 days in converting cotton to yarn. Finally having made 50 meters of yarn he spends another ten days in making the net. Thus, the processes are operated sequentially over time, the fisherman would take 30 man-days to complete the net. In other words the different stages of production exist over time, they do not co-exist in time. As the number of stages in producing a good is greater, the roundaboutness is greater, the time taken to produce the good is greater, in this approach.

*Cross Section Approach* : In this approach the different processes co-exist in time, they are simultaneously operated for instance, given the same technical datum if we wish to apply the cross section approach to the production of the net, firstly we have to assure certain proportions of cotton and yarn to exist as stock. For this purpose, suppose 2 days have to be spent on collecting cotton, i.e. to collect 5 kgs of cotton, and one day has to be spent on converting 2.5 kgs of cotton into 5 meters of yarn. For the cross section approach since the processes are operated simultaneously, 30 men are required. At this stage two forms of conceptualisation are possible. Either, we can imagine the emergence of an enterprising entrepreneur, who takes up the production of fishing nets, employs 30 workers and pays wages and produces nets to sell them at a profit to the fisherman or 30 fishermen decide to produce fishing nets by co-operative effort. For the sake of simplicity let us assume that fishermen are highly co-operative and enterprising, they decide to pool their man-hours together for the purpose of improving their lot by making a net each for themselves. Since their initial needs to operate the processes simultaneously is 2.5 kgs of cotton and 5 meters of yarn, the fishermen will have to spend 2 man-days on collecting cotton, one man day in converting half the cotton i.e. 2.5 kgs of cotton into 5 meters of yarn. Once 2.5 kgs of cotton and 5 meters of yarn are available, the three processes can be operated simultaneously, 10 fishermen will be engaged in collecting cotton, 10 fishermen will be making yarn and 10 others will be making the net.

Starting with a vector of inputs $\begin{pmatrix} 2.5 \\ 5 \\ 0 \end{pmatrix}$ the output vector at the end of the working day would be $\begin{pmatrix} 2.5 \\ 5 \\ 1 \end{pmatrix}$.

In this approach, cotton, yarn and net are made simultaneously so that at the end of a working day, not only a new net complete, the inputs of another net i.e. cotton and yarn are also produced. Hence, the inputs required for the next working day are available. In this interlinked system of processes, labour and goods make more goods in unit time. In this cross section approach to production once the goods are in required proportions, the production of intermediate and final goods are simultaneous. In fact once production is viewed as different processes co-existing in time, the concept of intermediate goods becomes irrelevant. Since all processes are worked simultaneously, all goods are produced at the same time and no good acts as an intermediate good between different stages of production *over time*. The thirty fishermen work for 30 days to make 30 nets, one net for each of them, after which, being equipped with a fishing net they go their separate ways.

In Bohm Bawerkian system as more roundabout methods are introduced, output is assumed to increase, though at a diminishing rate. Given the labour force and wage fund maximization of the rate of profit implies finding the optimum degree of roundaboutness. Bohm Bawerk was therefore in search of an optimum degree of roundaboutness where degree of roundaboutness is synonymous with capital intensity.

A measure of degree of roundaboutness, therefore, became important in the Bohm Bawerkian system. He saw the limitation of the absolute period of production as a measure of degree of roundaboutness, for it falls to reflect the uneven distribution of labour input over the period of production. For example,[2] consider Table, 1 where three different degrees of roundaboutness are shown with labour input (man days) evenly distributed over time. It can be observed that as absolute period of production is higher, total man-days input is lower, reflecting an assumption made by the Austrian School.

TABLE I

| Technique | t-3 | t-2 | t-1 | t | Labour input (man days) | Absolute period | Average period of production |
|---|---|---|---|---|---|---|---|
| A | — | — | 5 | 5 | 10 | 2 | 0.5 |
| B | — | 3 | 3 | 3 | 9 | 3 | 1.0 |
| C | 2 | 2 | 2 | 2 | 8 | 4 | 1.5 |

In technique A the average period of production is,

$$\frac{5 \times 1 + 5 \times 0}{10} = 0.5$$

In technique B the average period of production is,

$$\frac{3 \times 2 + 3 \times 1 + 3 \times 0}{9} = 1.0$$

While in technique C it is,

$$\frac{2 \times 3 + 2 \times 2 + 2 \times 1 + 2 \times 0}{8} = 1.5$$

It must be noted that in Bohm Bawerk's system as the structure of production is elongated, each unit of C-good is produced with less and less total labour. Hence, a higher degree of roundaboutness is compatible with lower labour input requirements. Due to this assumption and the use of simple interest to compound the value of inputs, as the rate of interest (rate of profit) is lower, more mechanised techniques become optimum. Further, under the Austrian set of assumptions, once a technique is discarded at a wage rate, it is discarded at all higher wage rates. Thus, the possibility of reswitching of techniques is ruled out, if labour is evenly distributed overtime, if a greater degree of roundaboutness implies less labour per unit of output and simple interest is used for compounding inputs over the period of production.

But when labour is unevenly distributed over time, Bohm Bawerk preferred the average period of production or average time over which labour is invested as a measure of roundaboutness of production. For example in Table II three methods[3] of producing a unit of C-goods are shown which have same absolute period of production (4) as well as total man hour requirement (8). However the methods differ as regards the distribution of labour input over time, technique A has an equal distribution of labour input, while technique B has more labour input at time 't' (present) compared to earlier periods and technique C, requires a greater dose of labour input in the year t-3, when production begins, than in the later years.

TABLE II

| Technique | t-3 | t-2 | t-1 | t | Total man hours | Period of production | Average period of production |
|---|---|---|---|---|---|---|---|
| A | 2 | 2 | 2 | 2 | 8 | 4 | 1.5 |
| B | 1 | 1 | 1 | 5 | 8 | 4 | .75 |
| C | 5 | 1 | 1 | 1 | 8 | 4 | 2.2 |

It can be seen that C is more roundabout than B when roundaboutness is measured through the average production period, which reflects its larger requirement of labour input in the earliest period of production than the later years.

If the assumptions made by Austrian Capital Theorists is relaxed, i.e., if labour is unevenly distributed over time, greater degree of roundaboutness does not imply less labour input for unit of output and if compound interest is used for computation, the possibility of reswitching of techniques emerges even within the simple production system where labour is the only input of production. For instance, consider[4] the following example where there are two techniques of production A & B.

| | t-3 | t-2 | t-1 | t |
|---|---|---|---|---|
| Technique A | 5 | 0 | 3 | 0 |
| Technique B | 0 | 0 | 4 | 1 |

At very low interest rates which implies very high wage rates, technique A becomes ineligible compared to technique B as it has a greater labour input, at very high interest rates technique A is ineligible as the 5 units of labour input required is valued at compound rate of interest over a longer period of production. Therefore, technique B emerges dominant at very low and very high interest rates, while technique A will be eligible over the middle ranges of interest rates. Thus, in this case as interest rates are higher, the order of eligible techniques would be B, A and back to B.

Knut Wicksell, a Swede, was influenced to a great extent by Bohm Bawerk's approach to the theory of capital. Wicksell's analysis of capital, therefore, is within the frame of the Austrian School.

*Knut Wicksell* : Wicksell's contribution to the theory of Capital is significant although like Bohm-Bawerk he chose to view capital goods from the lengthwise section, as saved up land and labour of earlier periods. Like J.B. Clark and unlike the classicals and Austrian Capital Theorists, Wicksell regarded capital as a factor of production. In general, he assumed that an increase in capital would increase output, though at a diminishing rate leading to a falling rate of return on capital.

Wicksell analysed a process of accumulation with capital deepening taking place overtime. He found that such an analysis requires a physical measure of capital, independent of distribution. He rejected the average production period as a measure of capital since valuation through average production period is not independent of the rate of profit, for the inputs have to be aggregated and compounded by the rate of interest over the average production period to arrive at the value of capital.

Wicksell was also aware of the limitation of a value measure of capital through its cost of production, for costs include interest costs, and if inputs are heterogeneous, aggregation involves relative prices which are not independent of distribution. It is clear that he was not in favour of deriving the value of capital goods from their own cost of production foı he writes "again, it is futile to attempt—with Walras and his followers—to derive the value of capital goods from their own cost of production or reproduction ; for in fact these costs of production include capital and interest, whereas our analysis of the laws of the cost of production has hitherto proceeded on the assumption that production is non-capitalistic. We should, therefore, be arguing in a circle".[5]

Thus, Wicksell was well aware of the limitations of the use of the average period of production as a value measure of capital and valuation of capital through cost of production approach.

However, his important contribution to the theory of capital lies in his analysis of the divergence of marginal productivity of capital and the rate of interest, when capital is social or aggregate capital.

Wicksell starts his analysis with a simple example[6] where a community is engaged in the production of wine alone. It exchanges wine for other commodities. Wicksell takes land, labour and capital as given. Further, the price of different vintages are given exogeneously in his example and the price of wine increases with the age of wine. Every year a fixed quantity of grape juice is produced in the community which is a product of labour alone. Therefore, price of grape juice, or zero year wine, $V_0$ per unit, consists of wages only. Wicksell assumes that the grape juice is stored so that it can be sold at a greater advantage. The length of time over which it will be stored would depend on the amount of existing capital in society, since the entire capital of society is in the form of stored wine. The money value of this capital is an unknown in his example, along with the community's equilibrium rate of interest, r and the price of grape juice $V_0$. Given the capital of the community there is a corresponding optimum period of production which Wicksell takes as 4 years. The prices of different vintages of wine being given, the rate of interest can be determined. For, if 3 year wine costs 90 shillings, 4 year wine 100 shillings and 5 year wine 110 shillings the rate of interest must be greater than 10%, otherwise 5 year wine will be as profitable as 4 year wine, violating the assumption of 4 year storage as optimum. Also the rate of interest must be less than 11% for, if not, it would be equally (or more) profitable to sell 3 year old wine. Thus, the rate of interest must be between 10 and 11%. Wicksell assumes the rate of interest to be 10.5%. Thus, given the optimum period of production and the prices of different vintages of wine the rate of interest is determined. Once the rate of interest is known the value of $V_0$ is determined by discounting the price of the 4 year old wine by the rate of interest for a period of 4 years, $V_0 = \frac{100}{(1.105)^4} = 67$ shillings.

Since the quantity of grape juice produced per year is fixed and given, total wages bill per annum is obtained by multiplying the quantity of grape juice produced by the price of grape juice ($V_0$).

In his model the circulating capital of the community would be "stored wine of four successive vintages." Its financial counterpart at the beginning of each year of account would be,

$$K_4 = q \times V_0 \, [1 + 1.105 + (1.105)^2 + (1.105)^3]$$

$$= q \times V_0 \frac{[(1.105)^4 - 1]}{0.105} = q \times \frac{67\,[(1.105)^4 - 1]}{0.105} = 314\, q$$

if q is the quantity of grape juice produced year after year. Since the whole of the community's capital existing at the beginning of the year is $K_4$ and the rate of interest is known (10.5%) the return to capital is calculated as 10.5% of $K_4$.

Next to disprove the theorem of Von Thunnen,[7] that marginal productivity of capital is equal to rate of interest, Wicksell considers an increase in the community's capital, which makes a 5 year storage optimum. He assumes that 6 year old wine costs 120 shillings per unit, in order to be able to calculate the rate of interest, by similar arguments he arrives at the rate of interest to be 9.5%. The price of new wine say $V'_0 = \frac{110}{(1.095)^5} = 69.88 \cong 70$ shillings. Thus, as the period of production is increased, the rate of interest is lower, wages bill per annum is higher. Further the community's total capital is $q\,\frac{69.88[(1.095)^5-1]}{0.095} = 422\,q$ shillings.

The rate of interest is determined with the help of the prices of different vintages of wine, given the community's capital which decides the optimum storage period. The rate of interest in other words "appears clearly in its simplest form as the marginal productivity of waiting." By elongating the period of production from 4 to 5 years the annual product in his example rises by 10% (as 4 year old wine costs 100 shillings and 5 years old wine costs 110 shillings). If six years storage is optimum the annual product rises by 9%. Therefore, he argues that the rate of interest lies between 9 and 10%, for a 5 year period of storage.

If the marginal productivity of capital is calculated it works out to be less than the interest rate determined by 'marginal productivity of waiting'.

For, in his example the increase in capital is 422 q—314 shillings = 108 q shillings, the corresponding increases in yield is 10 q shillings so that "the yield of the last portion of capital when taken with reference to the whole capital of community—reckoned in money (or C-goods)—yields a rate a little less than $9\frac{1}{4}\%$" $\left(\frac{10\,q}{108\,q} = 9\frac{1}{4}\%\right)$.

In Wicksell's examples wine of different vintages are aggregated in money terms so that when the period of production is made 5 years from 4 years, the value of capital is higher because the price of zero year wine goes up due to a fall in the rate of interest. The value of capital in money terms, when the period of production is raised to five years, is higher, which does not merely reflect the fact that one more year of vintage is stored but the earlier year vintages are revalued upwards because the price of grape juice is higher. Hence, the increase in the aggregate capital does not merely reflect physical increase but part of it is a mere revaluation of existing stock which has no impact in increasing the physical product. Wicksell explains the reason for the divergence of marginal productivity of capital and interest in pages 148-149 (much before he analyses with examples followed by formal mathematical proof).

"The explanation of this curious divergence is quite simple. Whereas labour and land are measured each in terms of its own technical unit (*e.g.* working days or months, acre per annum) capital, on the other hand, as we have already shown is reckoned in common parlance as a sum of exchange value—whether in money or as an average of products. In other words each particular capital good is measured by a unit extraneous to itself. The productive contribution of a piece of technical capital, such as a steam engine, is determined not by its cost but by the horse-power which it develops, and by the excess or scarcity of similar machines. If capital also were to be measured in technical units, the defects would be remedied and the correspondence would be complete".[8]

Wicksell supports his example by a mathematical model[9] depicting wine production under the assumption of "continuous production and sale." He uses a point input, point output production function for this purpose. He assumes that a fixed quantity of grape juice is produced everyday and equal quantity of mature wine is sold and at any moment of time, t-year vintages of wine are held as stock. If the price of one unit of wine is $V_0$ and one unit of mature wine is W, W is a function of time, as the value of wine increases with its age. With r representing the rate of interest at any moment of time Wicksell derives his first equation as,

$$W = V_0 e^{rt} \qquad \ldots\ldots (1)$$

The above equation can also be written as

$$V_0 = W e^{-rt} \qquad \ldots\ldots (1)$$

Where, $V_0$ is the present value of wine to be sold after 't' years. Then, Wicksell arrives at the conditions for maximising the value of $V_0$. In other words, an individual producer chooses an optimum 't' or storage period of wine so as to maximise $V_0$. The conditions for maximization are derived as follows :

From equation (1) Log $V_0$ = Log W −rt, differentiating with respect to,

$$t\ ,\frac{1}{V_0}\ \frac{dV_0}{dt}=\frac{W'}{W}-r$$

The necessary condition for maximum value is

$$\frac{dV_0}{dt}=0 \text{ or } \frac{W'}{W}=r \qquad \text{......(2)}$$

The sufficient condition is $\frac{d^2V_0}{dt^2}<0$

$$\textit{i.e.,}\quad \frac{d}{dt}\left(\frac{1}{V_0}\frac{dV_0}{dt}\right)=\frac{1}{V_0}\frac{d^2V_0}{dt^2}-\frac{1}{V_0^2}\left(\frac{dV_0}{dt}\right)^2$$

$$=\frac{W''\ W-W'W'}{W^2}<0 \qquad \text{......(3)}$$

Wicksell's fourth equation expresses the assumption that grape juice is continuously invested over the period t, which gives the value of K, by cumulated value of input at compound interest over the period of production which is, $K = V_0 \int_0^t e^{rt}dt$.

Since in equilibrium the discounted value of $W - V_0 = K$,

$$K=V_0\int_0^t e^{rt}\,dt=\frac{W-V_0}{r} \qquad \text{......(4)}$$

Further, by Logarithmic differentiation of equation (1) Wicksell arrives at eq. (5)

$$W=V_0\,e^{rt} \qquad \text{......(1)}$$

$$\text{Log } W=\text{Log } V_0+rt$$

$$\frac{W'}{W} = \frac{1}{V_0}\frac{\delta V_0}{\delta t} + r + t\,\frac{\delta r}{\delta t} \qquad ......(5)$$

As $r = \frac{W'}{W}$ from equation (2) substituting in equation 5

$$r = \frac{W'}{W} = \frac{1}{V_0}\frac{\delta V_0}{\delta t} + r + \frac{\delta r}{\delta t}\,t \qquad ......(5)$$

$$\text{or } r = \frac{1}{V_0}\frac{\delta V_0}{\delta t} + r + \frac{\delta r}{\delta t}\,t \qquad ......(5)$$

$$0 = \frac{1}{V_0}\frac{\delta V_0}{\delta t} + \frac{\delta r}{\delta t}\,t \qquad ...(5)$$

$$\text{or } \frac{1}{V_0}\frac{\delta V_0}{\delta t} = -\frac{\delta r}{\delta t}\,t = -t\,\frac{\begin{vmatrix} W & W' \\ W' & W'' \end{vmatrix}}{W^2}$$

$$\text{or} \quad \delta V_0 = -\,\delta r t\,V_0 = -\,V_0 t\,\frac{\begin{vmatrix} W & W' \\ W' & W'' \end{vmatrix}}{W^2}\,\delta t$$

$$\therefore \quad \delta V_0 = -\,V_0 t \delta r \qquad ......(5)$$

$$\text{or} \quad \frac{\delta V_0}{\delta K} = -\,V_0 t\,\frac{\delta r}{\delta K}$$

$$\frac{d V_0}{d K} = -\,V_0 t\,\frac{d r}{d K}$$

As $\begin{bmatrix} W & W' \\ W' & W'' \end{bmatrix} < 0$, a condition which is required for maximising $V_0$ from equation (5) it can be seen that $\delta V_0$, and $\delta t$ have the same sign, *i.e.* the direction of change in the period of storage is the same as change in the value of $V_0$. This means in Wicksell's Model when the storage period is increased the value of $V_0$ also increases. Further, from the same equation it can be seen that $\delta V_0$, $\delta r$ and $\delta$ r, $\delta t$ have opposite signs. Hence a lower r implies higher $V_0$ and a lower r implies higher t. Thus, as the period of storage is elongated (t is higher), r is lower $V_0$ is higher.

Also $$K = \frac{W - V_0}{r} \qquad \text{...... (4)}$$

$$\frac{\delta K}{\delta t} = \frac{r\,W' - Wr'}{r^2} - \frac{(V_0'\,r - r'\,V_0)}{r^2}$$

$$= \frac{r\,W' - Wr' - V'_0 r + r'V_0}{r^2}$$

from equation 5, $V''o = - tV_0\delta r$, substituting for $V'_0$ in the above equation we get,

$$\frac{\delta K}{\delta t} = \frac{r\,W' - W\,r' + tV_0\,\delta r \times r + r'\,V_0}{r^2}$$

$$= \frac{r\,W' - r'\,[W - V_0\,(1 + \delta\,rt \times r)]}{r^2} \text{ or}$$

$$\delta\,K = \frac{r\,W' - r'\,[W - V_0\,(1 + \delta rtr)\,\delta t}{r^2} \qquad \text{...... (6)}$$

Since $r'$ is negative and $W > V_0\,(1 + \delta tr)$ $\delta$ K and $\delta t$ have the same sign. In Wicksell's Model, therefore, an increase in capital necessarily implies an increase in the period of production.

Also from equation ...... (4)

$$K = \frac{W - V_0}{r}$$

or $$W = r\,K + V_0$$

$$\frac{dW}{dK} = r + K\frac{dr}{dK} + \frac{dV_0}{dK}$$

But $$\frac{dV_0}{dK} = - V_0 t \frac{dr}{dK}$$

$$\therefore \quad \frac{dW}{dK} = r + (K - V_0 t) \frac{dr}{dK}$$

In the above equation $\frac{dr}{dK} < 0$ and $K > V_0 t$ for $r > 0$,

$$\therefore \quad \frac{dW}{dK} < r$$

Thus, he proves that marginal productivity of capital is less than rate of profit, if K is 'Social Capital'.

It can be seen that Wicksell by starting with the necessary and sufficient condition for maximising the present value of wine sold after t-years, namely $\frac{W''}{W} = r$ and $\frac{\begin{vmatrix} W & W' \\ W' & W'' \end{vmatrix}}{W^2} < 0$ derives the result that increasing the period of storage increases the value of $V_0$ (and *vice versa*). Further, based on the same conditions, he proves that rate of interest and t are inversely related so also $V_0$ and r. Having proved the inverse relation between t and r, he proves that K and t are positively related. The results emerge as a logical conclusion from the conditions of wine production that are made by Wicksell, a highly simplified example of production in general, it can be seen, that even under highly simple conditions of production assumed, the marginal productivity of capital is proved to be less than rate of profit.

Wicksell while dealing with "Akerman's Problem"[10] found that marginal productivity of capital can be greater than rate of profit. Wicksell built a mathematical model where he introduced durable capital, he assumed two processes, a process where Axes are produced with labour alone, and a second process where labour and axes produce the consumption good. He assumed that when labour input is increased the axe's durability also increases. The production function that he used is similar to Cobb-Douglas production function. He set out to disprove the equality of marginal productivity and rate of profit and found that capital stock could also be devalued leading to Reverse Wicksell effect.

An observed increase in capital stock is made of up of two components ; (1) increase in physical capital, (2) a revaluation of capital stock. He found that the revaluation need not necessarily be upward.

Wicksell's analysis has great significance in capital theory, for, he found that the link between productivity of capital and the rate of profit cannot be established, since there can be no physical measure of aggregate capital, and a value measure includes a revaluation of stock, the separation of physical changes from price changes is not possible at the aggregate level, due to valuation and distribution being mutually dependant.

*Accumulation* : As mentioned earlier Wicksell considered a process of accumulation with capital deepening, where he assumed that as capital increases the output increases, but at a diminishing rate. Hence the marginal productivity of capital falls, leading to a following rate of profit in response to increase in capital. In his model of accumulation, he takes the aggregate capital stock at current prices as exogeneously given, along with N, the level of employment.

However, his own value theory illustrates that an aggregate concept of capital is not independent of distribution, and that in general, there is no relation between marginal productivity of capital and the rate of profit. If the value of aggregate stock of capital is not independent of distribution it cannot be taken to be exogeneously given. Thus, Wicksell's model of accumulation is undermined by his own theory of value, namely that marginal productivity of capital and rate of profit are unrelated when capital is "aggregate or social capital".

*J.B. Clark's Jelly Capital* : Clark Regards capital, which is distinct from capital goods as a factor of production on par with labour. Capital is "money invested in productive goods, the identity of which is for ever changing." The assumption of capital goods changing their form without effort, skill and time is crucial to his analysis, for it enables him to introduce the concept of measurement of marginal productivity of labour and capital. When an increment (notional) in capital is considered with labour constant, which is essential for the measurement of marginal product of capital, the physical counterpart of this capital fund is assumed to change its form instantaneously, so that a greater quantity of capital is associated with the same amount of labour force.[11]

As accumulation goes on "there are always made costlier machines, representing more capital and the product that comes from using them is a smaller fraction of its cost".[12] Hence, he argues as accumulation takes place the marginal product of capital falls and with it the earnings of capital, rate of interest, falls.

The rationale for making costlier machines as accumulation proceeds is explained by Clark "Everywhere do the forms of the capital show differences in earning power ; and the owners choose first the most productive forms, and later the less productive".[13] Thus, as additions are made to the capital fund the product increases but the rate at which it increases diminishes and the rate of interest is determined by the marginal product.

Clark's concept of static equilibrium which forms the basis of his analysis on capital is not a state of rest of an economy, achieved after, accumulation over time has been reduced to zero—the classical Stationary State. It is an analytical device where an economy is deemed to be in equilibrium with a given amount of accumulation. At any arbitrary point of time the quantities of factors are given. From this state of imaginary equilibrium national increments are considered for capital and the resulting addition to output is visualized to find capital's contribution at an imaginary margin. In his analysis equilibrium is compatible with any rate of accumulation (not necessarily zero).

However, though the setting is static, suspended equilibrium at any arbitrary point of time, the analytical device is said to be useful in highlighting the essential features of changes over time.

The analysis requires a value measure of capital, for existing stocks of capital at any moment of time have to be recorded to start with, in order that the impact of addition to capital on output may be analysed.

In the measurement of social capital and social product, Clark admits a value measure is necessary.[14] Rejecting the classical labour theory of value he develops instead, a subjective measurement in terms of "Effective Utility".[15]

The ultimate standard of value according to J.B. Clark is "the amount of social labour" that a good induces. "Goods for consumption induce social labour and are valuable in proportion to the amount of it that they severally draw out.[16] Clark has no difficulty in stretching his abstract concept of absolute value to measure capital, for he argues that "Capital creates consumers' wealth and thus indirectly induces social labour. The capital itself can be measured by means of this social labour which through its product, it induces".[17]

Clark's assumption of malleability of capital enables him to shift his argument from financial to physical, back and forth, as needed on the one hand, and to ignore the distinction between comparison of positions of equilibrium at a moment of time and accumulation over time.

Shift from one position of equilibrium to another, with a different set of capital goods, is a process of accumulation over time, accompanied by change in the form of capital goods. This can be brought about only by the time consuming dynamic process of building up stocks of a different set of capital goods, hitherto absent or inadequate in quantity. Such a process of change in capital structure implies investment decisions over time which in turn depends on 'foresight' of investors.

The assumption of malleability of capital which implies costless change in capital structure makes 'foresight' unimportant. Thus, Clark's assumption of instantaneous adjustment of capital structure leads him to conclude that comparisons of equilibrium positions with different capital structure would give insight to problems that are associated with accumulation over time with changing capital structure.

The malleability assumption also relegates the theory of value to the background. Although Clark develops an abstract theory of measurement of capital in terms of "social labour that it induces" he relies on market prices of capital for operational purposes. Further, his subjective value theory fails to integrate the financial and the physical world. In the absence of such an integration the constant shift of analysis from financial to physical and *vice versa* is invalid.

However, though Clark fails to integrate the theory of accumulation and the theory of value, he is not merely concerned with the theory of value, he is more concerned with the process of accumulation and the impact of accumulation on the rate of profit.

The forces that operate to bring about accumulation of stock in an economy, its impact on the other economic variables and the inter-relationship of the theory of accumulation and the theory of distribution have been the main concerns of all schools of Economics, Classical, Marxian, Neo-Classical and Keynesian.

However, with the advent of the Neo-Classical era (1870-1914), which began with the publication of the works of Jevons in England, Carl Menger in Austria and Leon Walras in Lausanne, with Alfred Marshall contributing independently on Jevon's lines, the emphasis shifted from the classical concept of accumulation to equilibrium analysis of supply and demand with zero accumulation—the stationary state. The dominance of neo-classical theory is explained, generally in terms of the inadequacies of the Classical School and on ideological basis.[18]

However, what is more important for the history of the development of the Theory of Capital is the fact that neo-classical theory had two distinct branches when it came to dominance, namely, the general equilibrium theory founded by Walras, elaborated by Pareto, and non-general equilibrium approach adopted by the Austrian and Marshallian Schools. In the Austrian School it was seen, that the analysis centred around the origin of capital and its accumulation over time. The Austrian and the Marshallian Schools developed the partial equilibrium branch of Neo-Classical Theory as an alternative to the General Equilibrium approach, as it was thought that the latter was too "General" to highlight specific issues. The marginal productivity theory emerged simultaneously in different countries, at least the essence of the later versions could be traced to Walras at Launsanne, Marshall and Wicksteed in

England, Wicksell in Sweden and Clark in the United States, at about the same time.[19]

It is this branch of neo-classical theory which led to the development of the concept of Aggregate Production Function, which was used as an analytical tool to tackle the theory of distribution by the application of the marginal principle to determine the factor prices. Thus, the marginal productivity theory emerged to determine the equilibrium factor prices through the marginal products of factors. In the neo-classical approach, therefore, the theory of distribution was just another aspect of the marginalist theory of value.

We have seen that Wicksell who regarded capital as a factor of production, tried to apply the marginal productivity principle to capital in order to determine the rate of profit. He found that when capital was Aggregate or Social Capital the marginal product of capital was not related to the rate of profit. Wicksell realised that even in simple cases of capital stock getting accumulated merely through passage of time it is not possible to value the stock of physical capital without knowing the rate of interest/rate of profit. Further, when value of Aggregate Capital is taken to be a factor of production, the marginal productivity of capital can either be less than or greater than the rate of profit. Contemporary and subsequent neo-classical theorists chose to ignore Wicksell's analytical insight. J.B. Clark (1847-1938) had no qualms about stating the 'law of final productivity' which 'tends to give to labour what labour creates, to the capitalists what capital creates, and to entrepreneurs (businessmen) what the co-ordinating function creates'.[20]

In early neo-classical theory interest or profit is said to arise due to the greater productivity of capitalistic mode of production and the consumers "time preference"—where the consumers are said to prefer present consumption to future consumption. Thus, there is an inherent conflict between their time preference and in the introduction of a more roundabout methods of production, which are more "fruitful" but require diversion of present consumption. However, the extra productivity gained by the use of capital intensive methods allows a premium to be paid to those who exchange present to future consumption—this premium is the rate of interest.

In the institution of capitalism, the workers who do not own property have a greater preference for present consumption and the capitalists advance wages and employ them in more round-about productive methods and "earn" a rate of profit in terms of the extra production that emerges due to the use of greater capital intensive methods. This extra production is the rate of return or rate of interest on wages (capital) advanced. Further, capital goods if used, will not vitiate the logic for it was argued that capital goods were only embodied wage fund. Thus, under the neo-classical set of assumptions capital a factor of production, is productive and capital deepening is associated with a higher output per man. With the assumption of "law of diminishing returns" or variable proportions, the increase in output per man was said to be at a diminishing rate, leading to an association of higher capital output ratio with higher capital per man. Further, due to the law of diminishing returns to the factor capital, as capital deepening takes place the return on capital falls and therefore brings about a fall in the rate of profit.

Capital deepening also increases the marginal product of labour and therefore the wage rate rises. From the positive relationship of W and K/L on the one hand, and the inverse relationship of r and K/L on the other an inverse relationship of W and r is derived. Thus, from the basic assumptions of the neo-classical theory a set of neo-classical propositions emerged and these became a part of received doctrine till Joan Robinson asked a very basic question as to what is K in neo-classical Aggregate Production Function.[21]

The basic neo-classical propositions get mathematical support through the concept of the production function when analysis is confined to a one commodity model. The one commodity model can be put in functional notation thus, $Q = F(K, L)$ where Q is the net output (corn), K is total capital (corn) and L total labour. If the function is assumed to be continuous, differentiable and linear homogeneous it can be reduced to per capita terms and can be drawn as a smooth curve. Using the mathematical axiom of linear homogeneous functions we get,

$$Q = F(\lambda K, \lambda L) \text{ where } \lambda$$

is a positive constant. If $\lambda = \frac{1}{L}$

$$\text{We get } \frac{Q}{L} = F\left(\frac{K}{L}, 1\right)$$

$$\text{or} \quad \frac{Q}{L} = f\left(\frac{K}{L}\right)$$

$$\text{or} \quad q = f(k) \text{ where } q = \frac{Q}{L}$$

$$\text{and } k = \frac{K}{L}$$

This Functional Relationship between output per man (q) and Capital per man $\left(\frac{K}{L}\right)$ is shown as a smooth curve on the two dimensional plane as in figure below, where k is measured in the x-axis and q on the y-axis.

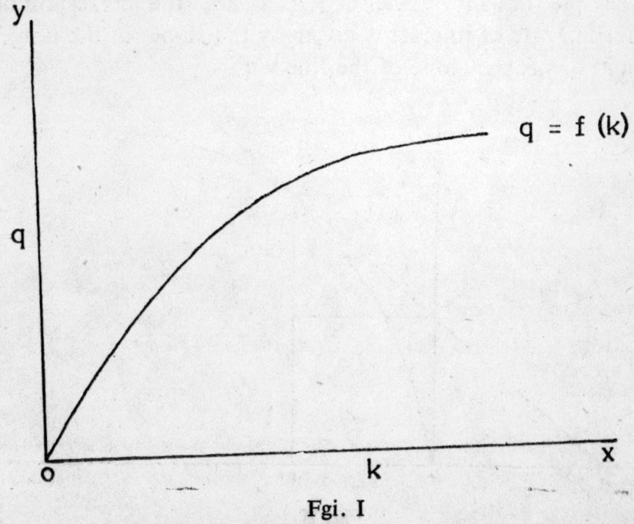


Fgi. I

The neo-classical assumptions get translated to mathematics, namely :

(1) f (o) = 0 which means when k = 0 so is q

(2) f′ (k) > 0 which means when k increases so does q

(3) f″ (k) < 0 which expresses the assumption of

diminishing returns to capital as a factor of production.

If in addition $f'(k) \longrightarrow \infty$ for $k \longrightarrow 0$ and
$f''(k) \longrightarrow 0$ as $k \longrightarrow \infty$

the production function is said to be 'well-behaved' which means the following neo-classical propositions which emerge from the assumptions hold.

(1) Wage rate and capital intensity are positively related ;

(2) Rate of Profit and capital intensity are negatively related ;

(3) Wage rate and rate of profit are negatively related ;

(4) Capital output ratio is inversely related to the rate of profit.

With the help of the Production Function drawn on per capita terms, the distribution relations can also be depicted. For example for any value of K/L = k*, the corresponding equilibrium rate of interest is given by the slope of the tangent drawn at q′ *i.e.* the slope of the line wq′.

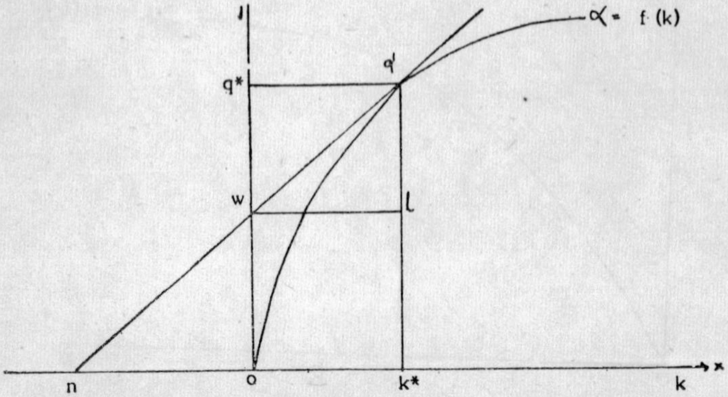


Fig. II

As $\frac{\partial Q}{\partial K}$, the partial derivate of Q with respect to K of the function Q = F (L, K) gives the marginal product of capital, which in equilibrium equals the return to the factor capital—the rate of interest, the slope of the tangent drawn at q corresponding to k* also equals the rate of interest as $\frac{\partial Q}{\partial K} = \frac{\partial q}{\partial k}$.[22]

The rate of interest $i = \frac{q' 1}{w1}$.

$$\text{or} \quad i = \frac{q' 1}{K^*}$$

$$K^* i = q' 1 = q^* w.$$

Hence, $q^* w$ represents the interest per worker, and $\frac{q^* w}{q^*}$ represents the share of interest in net income. As the production function Q = F (K, L) is assumed to be linear homogeneous. using Euler's theorem.

We get $Q = \frac{\partial Q}{\partial L} L + \frac{\partial Q}{\partial K} K$

$$\text{or} \quad \frac{Q}{L} = \frac{\partial Q}{\partial L} + \frac{\partial Q}{\partial K} \frac{K}{L}$$

As $\frac{\partial Q}{\partial K} = r$, the above equation becomes,

$$q = \frac{\partial Q}{\partial K} + rk$$

$$q - rk = \frac{\partial Q}{\partial L}$$

As $\frac{\partial Q}{\partial L}$ is the marginal product of labour, which in equilibrium, equals the wage rate, $\frac{\partial Q}{\partial L} = W = q - rk$.

Thus, the fifth neo-classical proposition, namely exhaustion of the product when factors are paid in accordance to their marginal products emerges from the assumption of constant returns to scale. In the diagram as Oq* is the total product per man and wq* is the interest per man, the wage per man is Oq* – q*w = Ow. It is obvious from the diagram that as $k \uparrow$ so does q, and as $k \uparrow r \downarrow$ and w increases. In order to predict the changes in relative shares, the concept of elasticity of substitution is used where,

$$\sigma = \frac{\text{relative change in k}}{\text{relative change in w/r}}$$

$$= \frac{d(k)}{k} \bigg/ \frac{d(w/r)}{w/r}$$

As elasticity of substitution depends on technology, it can vary.

Thus $\sigma \begin{matrix} > \\ = \\ < \end{matrix} 1$.

If $\sigma = 1$, it means that, in response to a, 1 per cent change in wage rate relative to the rate of interest, K will be substituted for L, such that the corresponding increase in K/L is just 1 per cent. Hence, the increase in K just offsets the fall in r, leaving the relative shares constant. Similar argument is used to predict the change in relative shares when $\sigma \neq 1$, namely $\sigma > 1$ decreases the share of labour, $\sigma < 1$ increases the share of labour.

The Aggregate Production Function can be used to rigorously state the assumptions of the Neo-Classical Model, and lend respectability by the use of mathematics to derive the basic neo-classical propositions. However, if heterogeneity of inputs is introduced, the Function fails to stand logical scrutiny. Inputs then are aggregates of heterogeneous commodities, and can be deemed homogeneous either by the assumption of malleability of capital or by the use of relative prices. J.B.

Clark chose to assume malleability of capital and with it assumed away the issues that arise in the Dynamic Process of accumulation over time. Swan took recourse to the Meccano set model to keep away the "Index number birds and Joan Robinson herself", so as to be able to use capital as a factor of production on par with labour.

The implications of the apparently harmless malleability of capital assumption is brought out explicitly by Swan himself, for he says to ward off the "Index number birds and Joan Robinson herself", one must assume "labour and land are homogeneous, man-hours and acres respectively, capital is made up of a large number of identical Meccano sets, which never wear out and can be put together, taken apart and reassembled with negligible cost or delay in a great variety of models so as to work with various combinations of labour and land, to produce products and to incorporate the latest technical innovations illustrated in successive issues of the Instruction Book. Output consists of goods (including Meccano sets) that are all produced and sold at constant price ratios amongst themselves, no matter how the rates of wages, rents and profits may vary *i.e.* they are all produced by similar (but continuously variable) combination of labour, land and capital, with similar efficiency, and under similar competitive conditions. Saving=Investment=Accumulation is the current output of Meccano sets, and can always be measured (by virtue of the constant price ratios) at a constant value per Meccano set in terms of peanuts or any other consumption product foregone etc."[23]

The difficulties in treating Aggregate Capital as a factor of production analysed by Wicksell was brought to the forefront by Joan Robinson by her article in 1954-55. Further, Joan Robinson argued that if capital is in value terms, since relative prices and distribution are mutually dependant, to get the value of Aggregate K, the rate of profit must be known, therefore, the Aggregate Production Function cannot be an analytical tool to determine rate of profit/rate of interest, through the marginal product of capital.

The Aggregate Production Function was also used as a tool to analyse the process of accumulation with capital deepening, for it depicts a series of Stationary States and the analytical insight gained by the comparison of the series of stationary states with different levels of capital intensity was said to be useful in gaining insight to the process of capital accumulation over time, Joan Robinson had strong objections to the application of results obtained by comparative static analysis to the Dynamics of accumulation over time, she writes—"When presented with the task of analysing a process of accumulation, the production function comes to grief in the failure to distinguish between comparisons of equilibrium positions and movements from one to another".[24]

For, if the different positions of equilibrium on the Production Function refer to economics with different physical capital stock, the process of movement along the production function implies change of capital structure, calling for Investment decisions over time, which in turn depends on 'foresight'. The assumption of malleability of capital which implies instantaneous and costless adjustment of capital stock, becomes essential to enable the applications of results obtained by comparative statics to accumulation with capital deepening over time. The Aggregate Production Function, therefore "comes to grief" as an analytical device to explain the relationships between crucial variables in the process of accumulation.

The neo-neo-classicals in defence of their theory of distribution came up with the argument that the invalidity of the concept of an Aggregate Production Function does not invalidate the marginal productivity theory of distribution.

They argued that in "core" neo-classical theory which is the General·Equilibrium Model developed by Walras, the Factor prices are in fact determined by the supply and Demand for Capital and Labour. Therefore, the marginal productivity theory of distribution still holds, and the logical invalidity of the Aggregate Production Function is of no consequence. Thus, the neo-neo-classicals when faced with an indefensible attack on the concept of the Aggregate Production Function took shelter in the basic neo-classical theory—the General Equilibrium Model.

However, Garegnani[25] argued that the Application of Supply and Demand Theory for Capital and Labour pose problems in the light of the theoretical possibility of capital reversing due to reswitching of techniques, a possibility which was examined by Joan Robinson, for the first time in 1956,[26] which was debated in 1966[27] and accepted as the general case rather than the perverse or exceptional case.

The causes of capital reversing are discussed in subsequent chapters, but to understand the basis for Garegnani's 'attack' on the marginal productivity theory of distribution, it must be noted that the acceptance of capital-reversing negates the neo-classical proposition, that rate of profit and capital intensity have inverse monotonic relationship. Therefore, the relationship in general, could be as in figure below.

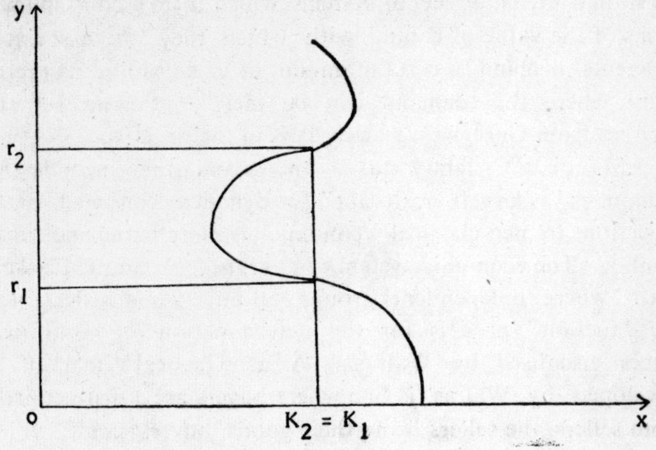


Fig. III

If rate of profit, capital relationship is to be viewed as a demand function of capital, it implies that as r, falls a new equilibrium is reached where the capital intensity is higher, this additional capital K represents the net savings that the community intended to save. This means a fall in r should necessarily imply a greater capital intensity, but the non-existence of an inverse-monotonic relationship shows that even for a drastic fall in r, the capital intensity may not be higher. For example, in figure when r falls from $r_2$ to $r_1$, the capital intensity in value terms is the same. Therefore, Garegnani, argues that it may not be possible to determine r, in general through the Supply and Demand for Capital.

In defence of neo-classical General Equilibrium Theory M.C. Howard[28] expresses the view that the demand curve used by Garegnani is applicable only to partial equilibrium theory, where a demand curve is a functional relationship between price of a commodity and the quantity demanded. The demand curve for value capital constructed by Garegnani cannot be used to demolish the general equilibrium theory, where commodities are physical entities independent of values. In general equilibrium frame-work, producers are not visualised to demand "value capital". However, Howard admits, to the question "Given a set of systems which form a continuum in terms of the value of capital with which they are associated, if agents demand a certain amount of value capital, is there a point where this demand can be met?",[29] the answer that emerges from Garegnani's analysis is in the negative.

J.M. Blatt[30] rightly takes the stand that neo-classical economics "is largely irrelevant" for dynamic economics. Blatt's objection to neo-classical economics is more basic and fundamental. The economic system, he argues, is most unlike a "fair" where independent groups of buyers and sellers meet, the "auction" process for the determination of equilibrium prices visualised by Walras. A neo-classical "market" as developed by Walras is one where buyers are a distinct group from sellers, the sellers bring their goods, buyers come with a certain quantum of purchasing power, even before the prices are determined through the "auction" process. As against this, in the alternative system developed by Sraffa, the quantities of input at the beginning of production and the output at the end of the production period called a "year" is sufficient to determine prices. In this system, buyers are also sellers, the total purchasing power of "buyers" depends on the price at which they can dispose off their product, and what is more important, supply determines demand. Instead of supply and demand operating to determine prices, in the Sraffa system, supply is given by what is produced in the earlier period and demand is determined by what is required for the next period of production to produce the same quantity of goods as were produced in the earlier period, ("last year"). Instead of prices influencing demand and supply, prices emerge from demand and supply, from the technical conditions of production so that the system can exchange goods or restore the input requirements of individual industries or sectors. As demand for intermediate goods is in the nature of derived demand, an analysis of the role played by technical condition of production in the determination of relative prices which help in restoring the input requirements of different industries in an interlinked system of production, will lead to a better understanding of the dynamic growth process. Though Sraffa conducts his analysis under the assumption of Stationary State, his analysis contains elements which could form the basis for the evolution of an alternative economic theory better, suited to comprehend the dynamic process of economic development.

We turn, therefore, in next and subsequent chapters to the Sraffa system, his solution to the Ricardian Puzzle, Switching and Reswitching of Techniques and a form of analysis which could lead to a better understanding of the role played by technological structures in accelerating the process of economic development.

## REFERENCES

1. Robert B. Ekelund Jr. and Robert F. Herbert : *A History of Economic Theory and Method*, (McGraw Hill, International Student Edition 1983), p. 288.
2. P.A. Samuelson : "A Summing Up", *Quarterly Journal of Economics*, (Vol. 80, 1966), pp. 568-83.
3. J.A. Kregel : The Theory of Capital, (Macmillan 1976), pp. 31-32.
4. *Ibid.*, fn. 2.
5. K. Wicksell : *Lectures on Political Economy*, Vol. I. (Routledge and Kegan Paul Ltd., Seventh Impression 1961), p. 149.
6. *Ibid.*, pp. 172-178.
7. *Ibid.*, pp. 177-178.
8. *Ibid.*, fn. 5.
9. *Ibid.*, pp. 178-180.
10. *Ibid.*, pp. 274-299.

11. J.B. Clark : *The Distribution of Wealth*, (Macmillan 1927), p. 183.
12. *Ibid.*, p. 185.
13. *Ibid.*, p. 186.
14. *Ibid.*, pp. 373-374.
15. *Ibid.*, p. 376.
16. *Ibid.*, p. 395.
17. *Ibid.*
18. Joan Robinson and Eatwell. An Introduction to Modern Economics, (TMH Edition 1974), pp. 34-35.
19. G.J. Stigler : *Production and Distribution Theories : The Formative Period*, (Macmillan 1949) p. 4.
20. J.B. Clark : *The Distribution of Wealth*, (Macmillan 1899), p. 3.
21. Joan Robinson : "The Production Function and the Theory of Capital" in *Collected Economic Papers*, (Vol. 2, Backwell 1965), pp. 114-31, First Published in *Review of Economic Studies*, Vol. 21, 1953-54, pp. 81-106.
22. M.C. Howard : *Modern Theories of Income Distribution*, (Macmillan, 1976), p. 98.
23. T.W. Swan : "Notes on Capital", *Capital and Growth*, Ed. by G.C. Harcourt and N.F. Laing, (Penguin 1971), p. 101, Excerpt from T.W. Swan, "Economic Growth and Capital Accumulation", *Economic Record*, Vol. 32, 1956, pp. 343-61.
24. *Ibid.*, fn. 21.
25. P. Garegnani : "Heterogeneous Capital, the Production, Function and the Theory of Distribution", *Review of Economic Studies*, (Vol. 37, pp. 407-36) Reprinted in *Hunt and Schwartz* (1972, pp. 245-91).
26. Joan Robinson, *The Accumulation of Capital*, (Macmillan 1956), Chapter 10.
27. Quarterly Journal of Economics, (Vol. 89, 1966).
28. *Ibid.*, fn. 22.
29. *Ibid.*, pp. 126-127.
30. J.M. Bhatt : *Dynamic Economic Systems—A Post Keynesian Approach*, (Wheatsheaf Books, Great Britain 1983), pp. 12-15.

## Chapter IV

# Sraffa and the Theory of Capital

*P. Sraffa* : Sraffa starts his analysis with a very simple model where processes of production depict commodities producing commodities, without the aid of machines, and the system of processes together produce just enough to replace the inputs which consist of means of production and the sustenance of workers. Sraffa shows that the system can exist period after period, for, a set of relative prices of the goods emerge from the technical relations which can bring about the original distribution of inputs between processes. Since there is no surplus in this model, the equations take the form, value of input=value of output. Hence, the number of equations would be 'n' if 'n' is the number of commodities produced in the system. However, the number of independent equations would be n—1 and therefore one of the commodities will have to be taken as a numeraire and the system then yields a set of viable relative prices.

Sraffa's simple model can be explained with the help of an example where only two goods $Q_1$ and $Q_2$ are produced. Consider the following two processes which produce just enough $Q_1$ and $Q_2$ to replace the inputs which include the means of subsistence.

| | Commodity I | Commodity II | | |
|---|---|---|---|---|
| Process I | $Q_1$ | $Q_2 \longrightarrow 3Q_1$ | | ...... (1) |
| Process II | $2Q_1$ | $5Q_2 \longrightarrow 6Q_2$ | | ...... (2) |
| | $3Q_1$ | $6Q_2$ | | |

It can be seen that the input requirements are $3Q_1$ and $6Q_2$ since mere replacement is going on in this model, only $3Q_1$ and $6Q_2$ are produced by the system. From these two processes, the price equations can be formed as,

$$Q_1P_1 + Q_2P_2 = 3Q_1P_1 \quad \text{...... (1)}$$

$$2Q_1P_1 + 5Q_2P_2 = 6Q_2P_2 \quad \text{...... (2)}$$

Where the rate of surplus R, is zero and prices are $P_1$ and $P_2$. Equations (1) and (2) are not independent. Therefore both $P_1$ and $P_2$ cannot be determined, as we have only one equation. If $P_1$ is taken as the numeraire of the system of prices, from equation (1) we have,

$$Q_1 + Q_2P_2 = 3Q_1$$

or,

$$Q_2P_2 = 2Q_1$$

$$P_2 = \frac{2Q_1}{Q_2}$$

Thus the relative prices are $2Q_1 : Q_2$. At the end of the production period, process (1) has $3Q_1$, it requires one unit of $Q_1$ and one of $Q_2$ for further production of $Q_1$ in the next period. Since $2Q_1 = Q_2$ is the relative price if the process retains one unit of $Q_1$ and exchanges $2Q_1$ for $Q_2$ its input requirements for the next period will be met. Industry 2 requires 2 units of $Q_1$ and 5 units of $Q_2$ as input. Out of 6 units of $Q_2$ if $5Q_1$ is retained and one unit of $Q_2$ be exchanged for $2Q_1$, the input requirements of the second Industry for production of $Q_2$ in the next period is met.

Thus, $2Q_1 = Q_2$ is the set of relative prices derived from technology.

Sraffa next introduces production with a surplus, where the wage rate and rate of profit are uniform in all the processes. The moment production with surplus is considered, a rationale for its distribution arises. If the system is to exist over time, the distribution of surplus must be in proportion to the means of production. Since the means of production are heterogeneous, although there are no machines used, prices are to be determined to aggregate the means of production. The relative prices cannot be determined unless the rate of profit is known, while the rate of profit cannot be computed without aggregating the heterogeneous inputs. Hence, the moment surplus exists in production, prices and rate of profit have to be determined by the set of equations simultaneously.

The existence of surplus also brings the possibility of some goods which appear in the surplus, which may not be used directly or indirectly in the production of every other good in the system. Thus, production with a surplus brings about the possibility of unequal ranking of goods, basic and non-basic goods emerge.

Finally Sraffa considers, production with a surplus, with wages paid post factum, if wages are paid out of net product, the quantity of labour required for each process has to be shown explicitly. Hence, the equation takes the form, for each commodity produced, value of inputs $\times$ coefficient profit, profit $+$ wages bill $=$ value of output. Sraffa thus arrives at K equations for the K goods that are produced in K processes. The net product of the system is obtained by substracting item by item, the means of production used. Sraffa obtains an additional equation by setting the value of the net product equal to unity. The system consists of $K+1$ equations, and $K+2$ variables, namely K prices, the wage rate and the rate of profit r. Therefore, by expression of wage and K prices in terms of the composite commodity, Sraffa develops a set of simultaneous independent equations, which can be solved for K prices and r given w, or K prices and W given r. Since wage is expressed in terms of the value of the net product, when wage is given notional values ranging from 0 to 1, they represent fractions of national income. He considers notional changes in wages and its effect on prices and rate of profit holding the methods of production constant.

*Mathematical Approach to the Sraffa System* : L. Pasinetti presents the Sraffa system using Matrix algebra.[1] His approach lends considerable clarity to the Sraffa system. An attempt is made therefore, to follow his approach and highlight the essence of the Sraffa system with the help of simple examples based on Matrix algebra.

Sraffa presents a sub-economy where inputs of an industry are depicted as a row, thus if wheat and iron are the only two goods produced in an economy, where inputs consist only of working capital, the format of depiction is as follows,

| | W | I | | W | I |
|---|---|---|---|---|---|
| W | 20 | 10 | ——→ | 40 | — |
| I | 5 | 20 | ——→ | — | 30 |

In order to facilitate the use of Matrix algebra the above sub-economy can be depicted as,

| | W | I | | W | I |
|---|---|---|---|---|---|
| W | 20 | 5 | ——→ | 40 | 0 |
| I | 10 | 20 | ——→ | 0 | 30 |

In this case, the column vector represents the inputs of an industry (L.H.S.), the coefficient matrix A can be derived as follows,

$$\begin{array}{c} \\ W \\ I \end{array}\begin{array}{c} \quad W \quad\quad I \\ \begin{bmatrix} \frac{20}{40} & \frac{5}{30} \\ \frac{10}{40} & \frac{20}{30} \end{bmatrix} \end{array} = A = \begin{bmatrix} 0.50 & .17 \\ 0.25 & 0.70 \end{bmatrix}$$

If, in addition to the coefficient matrix A, if the labour requirement is known per unit of output in each industry as $a_{31}$ and $a_{32}$ the technological information is complete, consisting of,

$$A = \begin{vmatrix} a_{11} & a_{12} \\ a_{21} & a_{22} \\ a_{31} & a_{32} \end{vmatrix}$$

Where the 3rd row represents the labour inputs. The price equations in this system are,

$$(a_{11}P_1 + a_{21}P_2)\ (1+r) \ + \ a_{31}W = P_1 \qquad \ldots\ldots (1)$$

$$(a_{12}P_1 + a_{22}P_2)\ (1+r) \ + \ a_{32}W = P_2 \qquad \ldots\ldots (2)$$

Where W is the wage rate and r the rate of profit, $P_1$, $P_2$ the prices of a unit of wheat and iron. In matrix notation the two equations can be represented as,

$$PA\ (1+r) + a_{31}\ W = P \qquad \ldots\ldots (I)$$

where P is a row vector.

Thus, we get two equations corresponding to the goods produced in the system, the unknowns are W, r, $P_1$ and $P_2$. It is clear that given W, r and relative price can be determined or given r, W and relative prices can be determined from the two equations. In other words, relative prices can be determined from the equations based on technology, given the distribution.

Now consider the system of equations,

$$(I-A)\ Q=Y \quad \text{where } A = \begin{bmatrix} a_{11} & a_{12} \\ a_{21} & a_{22} \end{bmatrix},\ Q = \begin{bmatrix} Q_1 \\ Q_2 \end{bmatrix}$$

$Q_1$ is the total quantity of wheat produced $Q_2$, the total quantity of Iron produced in the economy. $Y = \begin{bmatrix} Y_1 \\ Y_2 \end{bmatrix}$

where $Y_1$ is the surplus of wheat, $Y_2$ the surplus of Iron. It must be noted that since Sraffa is dealing with a stationary state $Y_1$, $Y_2$ are consumed.

Now $(I-A)\ Q = Y$ can be put as,

$$Q_1 = a_{11}Q_1 + a_{12}Q_2 + Y_1 \quad \ldots\ldots (1)$$

$$Q_2 = a_{21}Q_1 + a_{22}Q_2 + Y_2 \quad \ldots\ldots (2)$$

Or $$Q = (I-A)^{-1}\ Y$$

If $$(I-A)^{-1} = \begin{bmatrix} \alpha_{11} & \alpha_{12} \\ \alpha_{21} & \alpha_{22} \end{bmatrix}$$

$$\begin{bmatrix} Q_1 \\ Q_2 \end{bmatrix} = \begin{bmatrix} \alpha_{11} & \alpha_{12} \\ \alpha_{21} & \alpha_{22} \end{bmatrix} \begin{bmatrix} Y_1 \\ Y_2 \end{bmatrix}$$

Any element of the A matrix say $a_{ij}$, represents $i^{th}$ commodity needed in the $j^{th}$ industry to produce one unit of the $j^{th}$ good, *i.e.* (A) gives the direct requirements of commodities to produce commodities, $\alpha_{ij}$ on the other hand, an element of the inverse matrix, $(I-A)^{-1}$, represents physical quantities of the $i^{th}$ commodity needed in the economic system as a whole to produce one unit of $j^{th}$ commodity for final use. $\alpha_{ij}$ represents both direct and indirect, inputs required to produce one unit of $j^{th}$ commodity for final use. The inverse matrix $(I-A)^{-1}$ represents therefore, direct and indirect requirements of commodities to produce the vector of commodities for final use.

A column vector of the $(I-A)^{-1}$ matrix, say $j^{th}$ column, represents a heterogeneous set of commodities in general, which are necessary in total in order that one physical unit of $j^{th}$ commodity may be available for final use.[2]

*The Extreme Cases* : When the wage is unity, the entire net product consists of wages, in this case prices turn out to be proportional to quantities of labour, further if the wage is taken as the numeraire, prices are equal to quantities of labour. Thus, when the rate of profit is zero relative prices coincide with labour theory of value.[3]

In equation I, *i.e.* $PA(1+r) + a_{3i} W = P$

$$\text{if } r = 0 \text{ we get } PA + a_{3i} W = P$$

$$\text{or } a_{31} W = P(I-A)$$

$$\text{or } P(I-A) = a_{3i} W$$

$$P = a_{3i} W (I-A)^{-1}$$

$$= a_{3i} (I-A)^{-1} W \qquad \text{......(II)}$$

The inverse matrix represents physical quantities of commodities used both direct and indirect, in the economy to get one unit of vector of commodities for final use $a_3$. $(I-A)^{-1}$ gives the scaler product of these commodities and the corresponding labour coefficients, which gives the total quantity of labour used in the economic system as a whole. Therefore, if $W=1$ prices are equal to physical quantities of labour. For example $P_1 = a_{31} \alpha_{11} + a_{32} \alpha_{21}$ where $a_{31}$ and $a_{32}$ are direct labour coefficients, $\alpha_{11}$ and $\alpha_{21}$ are the commodity requirements of sector I, both direct and indirect in order to produce one unit of commodity I for final use.

*Wage Out of Surplus is Zero* : If goods that are needed for subsistence is included as inputs in production, as a technical datum and if wage paid out of the surplus is zero, prices become proportional to the means of production.

*Case II* : If $W = 0$ rate of profit is maximum *i.e.* $r = R$. In this case Eq. I takes the form,

$$PA(1+R) = P \qquad \text{......(II)}$$

$$\text{or, } P - PA(1+R) = 0$$

$$\text{or, } P[I - A(1+R)] = 0$$

The system yields as many equations as the commodities produced. In the two goods case, therefore, there are two equations, the unknowns of the system are $P_1$, $P_2$ and R. Therefore R and relative prices can be determined. Further, as W = 0 the surplus accrues to the profit earners *i.e.* Surplus = Profits. Hence, surplus/profits are distributed between processes proportionately to means of production or (working capital). Pasinetti calls this case as Pure Capital Theory of Value.[4]

*General Case* : Between these two extreme cases of distribution, lies the general case where the rate of profit is neither at technical maximum (W=0) or zero. When the rate of profit is greater than zero, the quantities of indirect labour become relatively more important compared to the quantities of direct labour, as profits have to be imputed over longer time, if production is viewed from the length-wise section, where different layers of production do not coexist in time. In this case the proportionality between prices and quantities of embodied labour no longer holds true. In the general case relative prices are governed both by the embodied labour and the level of the rate of profit. Therefore, even when the technical coefficients, remain constant, relative prices will in general change, with change in the rate of profit.

Sraffa demonstrates the role of the level of rate of profit in the determination of relative prices with the method of production held constant in the chapter "Reduction to dated quantities of labour".[5] The approach to relative prices is through their cost of production both direct and indirect, where the means of production of a commodity A is replaced by their means of production and labour expended by an year earlier ; the profit factor attached to each of these terms differ, the means of production are compounded over 2 years, $(1+r)^2$ while labour expended is compounded over a single year $(1+r)$ as labour is paid post factum in his system. These means of production and labour are replaced by their means of production and labour expended, suitably compounded by profit factor $(1+r)^3$ and $(1+r)^2$. By repeating this operation, Sraffa arrives at the reduction equation for the commodity A, which is an infinite series.

$$L_a w + L_{a_1} w (1+r) + \ldots L_{a_n} w (1+r)^n + \ldots = AP_a$$

It is obvious from the above equation, that as the rate of profit changes the terms of the equation are affected by two opposing elements, the wage and the rate of profit. Further terms which belong to different dates get affected by the level of rate of profit differently. Thus, the value of the elements of the equation depend on the relative strength of the two opposing forces acting on it, which in turn depends on the level of rate of profit and the remoteness of an element in time.

Therefore the value of the commodity, A will be different at different levels of the rate of profit given the method of production. If another commodity B is considered, by computing the reduction equation for it, by similar argument B's value would in general depend on the distribution of labour over its many layers of production and the level of the rate of profit. In other words, the value of commodity, B will be different at different rates of profit, although its method of production is constant. Sraffa, therefore, considers the case of two different commodities produced with the same amount of labour, but differently distributed over time, to demonstrate the logical possibility of price reversals between the two commodities, without any change in their methods of production.

Assuming "one of them 'a', has an excess of 20 units of labour applied 8 years before, whereas the excess of the other 'b' consists of 19 units employed in the current year and 1 unit bestowed 25 years earlier."[6] Sraffa arrives at the equation which represents the difference between their prices as a function of the rate of profit *i.e.*,

$$P_a - P_b = 20W (1+r)^8 - [19W + W (1+r)^{25}].$$

When $P_a - P_b$ is measured on Y-axis and r, the rate of profit on the X-axis, the figure reproduced below is obtained. It is clear from the figure that $P_b$ rises relatively to $P_b$ for values of r between 0 to 9 percent falls between r = 9 percent and r = 25 percent only to rise again between 22 percent to 25 percent, rate of profit.

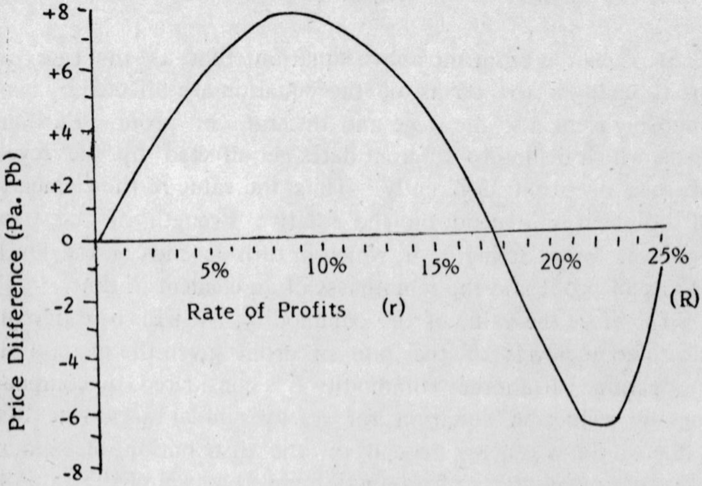


Fig. I

Sraffa thus demonstrates reversals in the direction of movement of relative prices with the method of production constant. He conclusively proves, therefore, that there can be no "notion of capital as a measurable quantity independent of distribution and prices"[7] by his example where reversals in the direction of prices occur, without a change in the methods of production in response to a notional change in the rate of profit.

Thus, Sraffa's analysis destroys the neo-classical theory of distribution, where capital as an aggregate measure enters the production function and the rate of profit is determined by the marginal product of capital, as there can be no aggregate measure of capital independent of distribution.

However, analysis of price reversals within a given technique of production need not necessarily involve the lengthwise approach to the production process, where the different layers of production have to be traced backwards in time with the help of "dated labour".

The analysis of price reversals within a given technique of production, where a technique is a set of processes co-existing in time, which retains the essential characteristics of technology, such as heterogeneous capital goods, fixed man to machine ratio, and interdependence of processes in production is possible and more relevant in the context of modern technological production.[8]

While the assumption of uniform wage in all processes of production within a technique allows the classification of techniques in terms of Wicksell structures,[9] the cause of the price reversals really lies in the difference in the organic composition of capital between different processes that form a technique of production.

The organic composition may differ due to technical reasons like difference in productivity of machines which has an impact on its value, and hence even at uniform wage, the value of capital to wage ratio may be different between processes of organic composition may be different due to wage rate being different between processes or raw material input being different in value as between processes or due to a combination of any two or all three of these.

Whenever organic composition differs between processes, relative prices change in response to a difference in wage rate, the proportion of value of capital to wage rate gets affected differently, in different processes, due to the initial difference in organic composition. Hence, if rate of profit is to be uniform, relative prices have to adjust to the new capital wage ratio. In case the structure of organic composition is complex between processes, price reversals are inevitable.

For example, consider the following technology, where there are four departments is the capital goods sector, and a process for the production of the consumption good C (Corn). Wage is uniform, and paid in advance of production, in terms of Corn which enters the input-output matrix as a surrogate for labour. Further, assumptions are that workers consume their entire wage paid in advance of production, and entrepreneurs do not consume out of their profits. Workers do not get a share in the surplus.[10]

TECHNOLOGY A

| Men | | | | | | | | | | |
|---|---|---|---|---|---|---|---|---|---|---|
| C | $e_1$ | $e_2$ | $e_3$ | $e_4$ | | C | $e_1$ | $e_2$ | $e_3$ | $e_4$ |
| W | 1 | 0 | 0 | 0 | ——→ | 25 | 1 | 0 | 0 | 0 |
| W | 0 | 1 | 0 | 0 | ——→ | 0 | 16 | 1 | 0 | 0 |
| W | 0 | 0 | 1 | 0 | ——→ | 0 | 0 | 1 | 1 | 0 |
| W | 0 | 0 | 0 | 1 | ——→ | 0 | 0 | 0 | 14 | 1 |
| W | 0 | 0 | 0 | 1 | ——→ | 0 | 0 | 0 | 0 | 6+1 |

For the above technology the price equations are,

$$(W+P_1)R = 25 + P_1 \quad \ldots\ldots \quad (1)$$

$$(W+P_2)R = 16P_1 + P_2 \quad \ldots\ldots \quad (2)$$

$$(W+P_3)R = P_2 + P_3 \quad \ldots\ldots \quad (3)$$

$$(W+P_4)R = 14P_3 + P_4 \quad \ldots\ldots \quad (4)$$

$$(W+P_4)R = 7P_4 \quad \ldots\ldots \quad (5)$$

Where W is the uniform wage rate, R the coefficient of profit, $P_1$, $P_2$, $P_3$ and $P_4$ are prices of equipment, $e_1$, $e_2$, $e_3$, $e_4$ in terms of the price of the C-good $P_o$. These equations are solved for R = 3.5, 4.09, and 4.5 and the relative prices are tabulated in the Table below. It can be observed that the prices of $P_1$ and $P_3$ cross when R = 4.09.[11] It can be observed from the table that $P_4$ rises in terms of $P_0$ when R is changed to 3.5 to 4.09 and then falls when R takes values from 4.09 to 4.5.

TABLE I

| R | $P_0$ | $P_1$ | $P_2$ | $P_3$ | $P_4$ |
|---|---|---|---|---|---|
| 3.5 | 1 | 1.222 | 6.112 | .737 | 1.220 |
| 4.09 | 1 | 1.433 | 6.070 | .614 | 1.433 |
| 4.5 | 1 | 1.447 | 5.616 | .601 | 1.404 |

*Invarient Measure of Value* : Sraffa develops his "invarient measure of value" systematically and carefully. Having analysed the conditions under which a commodity's value is invarient with respect to distribution, he develops a system of processes, from the actual economic system, so that goods produced and means of production are in the same proportion, which he calls the standard system. The standard system enables him to arrive at a ratio R called the "Standard Ratio" which is the standard net product by means of production. As in the standard system, the standard net product and means of production consist of goods in the same proportion, this ratio R remains invarient to distribution. For, even if prices change with change in r, the ratio is not altered since any set of prices will affect the numerator and the denominator of the ratio to the same extent and leave the ratio unchanged. From the standard system Sraffa also derives the Standard Commodity.

If the scale of operation of the standard system is such as to use the labour that is used in the actual system, the standard system yields a particular standard Net Product, a vector where goods are in specified proportions. This vector of Net Product is called by Sraffa, Standard Net Product. This vector of goods is also called Standard Commodity, it should be noted that a multiple or fraction of this vector of Net Product would still be the 'Standard Commodity', for the standard commodity is a set of goods which are in a certain proportion, the proportion in which inputs and outputs appear in the Standard system, where total output and means of production are in the same proportion. Sraffa then proves the linear relationship between the rate of profit and the wage rate in the Standard system, where wage is in terms of the Standard Commodity paid from the surplus, and where the value of Net Product of the Standard system is taken to be the numeraire, thus the standard commodity becomes the numeraire of the price system.

The linear relation between the wage rate and the rate of profit thus emerges in the equation $r = (1—W) R$. In the standard system, as profits by total capital (means of production) are in the same proportion, the rate of profit is invarient to prices and is a physical ratio, and R the Standard Ratio, which is the ratio of Net Product to means of Production of the Standard system, is also invarient to prices as the numerator and denominator are both vectors in the same proportion. Thus, Sraffa with the help of his concept of standard system. standard ratio and composite commodity in terms of which wage is paid, arrives at a linear relation between wage rate[12] and rate of profit, a relation which isolates the impact of change in relative prices due to change in distribution.

Sraffa proves that the relation holds for the actual system as well, though only in value terms, if wage is paid in terms of composite commodity. The Standard System and the actual system consist of the same processes of production, and the standard system differs from the actual system only in goods not being produced in specified proportions, namely, that total output and means of production are in the same proportion. Hence, in the actual system although goods are not in standard proportions, if out of the net product valued at Standard Prices, value of wage paid in standard commodity is subtracted, the ratio of profits in value terms to the value of means of production of the actual system will still be related linearly to the Standard Ratio. This is because, the price system is independent of the system of physical quantities.[13]

Further, Sraffa's standard commodity has been proved to be invarient with respect to prices as its many layers of production reveal the same ratio of labour to means of production.[14] Thus, when used as a numeraire, it allows distribution relation to be studied in isolation, without affecting the linear relation due to the influence of the rate of profit on the value of the numeraire commodity.

The Standard Commodity is also the unit of measurement of the quantity of capital in the Sraffa system, so that a difference in value of capital is independent of changes in the value of the numeraire commodity, since the standard commodity is invarient to distribution changes.

*General Case* : In general, r is neither zero nor maximum (*i.e.* $W=0$), r lies between $0 < \bar{r} < R$. Equation I takes the form,

$$PA(1+\bar{r}) + a_{3i}W = P \qquad \ldots\ldots \quad I$$

In the general case, prices are dependant on technical coefficients as well as the level of the rate of profit, $\bar{r}$. In this case whenever W changes, $\bar{r}$ changes and the relative prices change. Therefore, the relationship between the wage rate and rate of profit is highly complicated, the W-r curve, in general, will not be a straight line.

For example consider $\gamma$ certain physical Net Product (I—A) Q. As long as we consider share of this net product between wage earners and profit earners, there is no problem but once we introduce the concepts of rate of profits and wage rate complications arise. If net product per man is made equal to one, wage rate w coincides with share of wages W.[15] But the moment rate of profit is introduced into the analysis relative prices cannot be avoided. In this case changes in the rate of profit will reflect both the changes in w and changes in the relative prices.

The reason for relative prices to change, in general, when r or w changes, given the technique of production, is the difference in organic composition between different processes that constitute a technique. Whenever, the ratio of value of capital to wage rate differs between processes, a given change in w affects different processes in different proportions. If a uniform rate of profit is to prevail in all the process, relative prices must adjust. Thus, a change in relative prices is inevitable.

*Special Case* : In case the organic composition is the same in all the processes of a technique, relative prices will remain constant when notional changes are considered in w or r. In this case w-r relationship will be a straight line, for w-r relationship reflects only income distribution phenomenon, free from changes in values.

In general, w-r relationship also reflects changes in price structure, apart from changes in distribution, Sraffa's problem centres around how to isolate the distribution phenomenon from changes in value.

*2nd Special Case* : Sraffa examines the case of same organic composition between processes leading to relative prices being independent of distribution, dismisses it as a rare case and constructs instead a standard system. By imposing the condition that the rate of surplus of each commodity should be the same within a system of processes, he arrives at a system where the proportion in which goods are produced, is the same as the proportions in which the means of production are, which he calls the Standard System.

The uniform rate of surplus of commodities condition yields physical quantities of Q so that the composition of Q produced, is the same as the goods used as means of production. It follows that total product—Means of production, which is the Net product of the system is also in the same proportion.

However, by organising production such that the rate of surplus of each commodity in the system in the same, gives only the structure of production *i.e.*, determines the relative quantities of goods produced but the level of production is indeterminate. If the level of production is also to be determined, an additional relation is required. Sraffa therefore, takes the total labour force in the economy to be given, to get a system of n+1 equations in n+1 unknowns, R and n physical quantities corresponding to n goods produced.

Consider the simple two goods model, where $Q_1$ and $Q_2$ are produced in a system, $Y_1$, $Y_2$ are the corresponding quantities used for final consumption. The means of production would, therefore, be $Q_1—Y_1$ and $Q_2—Y_2$.

If $A = \begin{bmatrix} a_{11} & a_{12} \\ a_{21} & a_{22} \end{bmatrix}$ is the inter-industry coefficient matrix, we get the equations,

$$a_{11}\, Q_1 + a_{12}\, Q_2 + Y_1 = Q_1 \qquad \dots (1)$$

$$a_{21}\, Q_1 + a_{22}\, Q_2 + Y_2 = Q_2 \qquad \dots (2)$$

Now let $R_1$ and $R_2$ be the rate of surplus in process (1) and (2) respectively.

$$R_1 = \frac{Y_1}{Q_1 - Y_1}, \qquad R_2 = \frac{Y_2}{Q_2 - Y_2}$$

$$\text{or } R_1 (Q_1 - Y_1) = Y_1$$

$$R_1 Q_1 = Y_1 + R_1 Y_1$$

$$= (1+R) Y_1$$

$$\text{or } Y_1 = \frac{R_1 Q_1}{1+R_1}$$

$$Y_2 = \frac{R_2 Q_2}{1+R_2}$$

Substituting for $Y_1$ and $Y_2$ in equations (1) and (2) we get,

$$a_{11} Q_1 + a_{12} Q_2 + \frac{R_1 Q_1}{1+R_1} = Q_1 \qquad \text{... (1)}$$

$$a_{21} Q_1 + a_{22} Q_2 + \frac{R_2 Q_2}{1+R_2} = Q_2 \qquad \text{... (2)}$$

$$a_{11} Q_1 + a_{12} Q_2 - \frac{Q_1}{1+R_2} = O \qquad \text{... (1)}$$

$$a_{21} Q_1 + a_{22} Q_2 - \frac{Q_2}{1+R_2} = O \qquad \text{... (2)}$$

In matrix notation the two equations can be put as,

$$\begin{bmatrix} a_{11} - \dfrac{1}{1+R_1} & a_{12} \\ a_{21} & a_{22} - \dfrac{1}{1+R_2} \end{bmatrix} \begin{bmatrix} Q_1 \\ Q_2 \end{bmatrix}$$

As these are homogeneous equations, the necessary condition for a solution is,

$$\begin{vmatrix} a_{11} - \dfrac{1}{1+R_1} & a_{12} \\ a_{21} & a_{22} - \dfrac{1}{1+R_2} \end{vmatrix} = 0$$

Therefore, both $R_1$ and $R_2$ cannot be exogeneously given ; one of them can be, say $R_2$. Therefore, $R_1$, $Q_1$, $Q_2$ are the unknowns. As there are two equations and three unknowns, only structure of production can be determined. If the scale of operation is to be determined one more equation is required. Sraffa takes $\bar{Q}_n$ as given, *i.e.* total quantity of labour available in the economy.

Consider the example : $2Q_1\ 2Q_2 \longrightarrow 8Q_1$ Process (1)

$2Q_1\ 5Q_2 \longrightarrow 8Q_2$ Process (2)

If $\lambda_1$ and $\lambda_2$ determine the structure such that the rate of surplus of $Q_1$, $Q_2$ is the same, in other words if the above system is to be converted into Sraffa's Standard system,

$$2Q_1\lambda_1\ 2Q_2\lambda_1 \longrightarrow 8Q_1\lambda_1$$

$$2Q_1\lambda_2\ 5Q_2\lambda_2 \longrightarrow 8Q_2\lambda_2$$

$$(2Q_1\lambda_1 + 2Q_1\lambda_2)\ (1+R) = 8Q_1\lambda_1 \qquad ...(1)$$

$$(2Q_2\lambda_1 + 5Q_2\lambda_2)\ (1+R) = 8Q_2\lambda_2 \qquad ...(2)$$

If the rate of surplus are to be the same we get,

$$\frac{8Q_1\lambda_1}{2Q_1\lambda_1 + 2Q_1\lambda_2} = \frac{8Q_2\lambda_2}{2Q_1\lambda_1 + 5Q_2\lambda_2}$$

$2\lambda_1 = \lambda_2$ *i.e.* we get only the relative quantities of $Q_1$, $Q_2$. Now suppose total labour force is 10 Units, and 4 units are needed in process 1 and 6 units in process (2) we get the additional equation as $\frac{4}{10}\lambda_1 + \frac{6}{10}\lambda_2 = 1$

Since $2\lambda_1 = \lambda_2$ ; $\frac{4}{10}\lambda_1 + \frac{6}{10} \times 2\lambda_1 = 1$

$$\frac{16\lambda_1}{10} = 1$$

$$\lambda_1 = \frac{10}{16} = \frac{5}{8}$$

$$\lambda_2 = \frac{5}{4}$$

Using $\frac{5}{8}$, $\frac{5}{4}$ as multipliers the processes become,

$$2 \times \frac{5}{8} Q_1 \quad 2 \times \frac{5}{8} Q_2 \longrightarrow 8Q_1 \times \frac{5}{8} \qquad \ldots(1)$$

$$2 \times \frac{5}{4} Q_1 \quad 5 \times \frac{5}{4} Q_2 \longrightarrow 8Q_2 \times \frac{5}{4} \qquad \ldots(2)$$

*or,*

$$\frac{5}{4} Q_1 \quad \frac{5}{4} Q_2 \longrightarrow 5Q_2 \qquad \ldots(1)$$

$$\frac{5}{2} Q_2 \quad \frac{25}{4} Q_2 \longrightarrow 10Q_2 \qquad \ldots(2)$$

$$\overline{\frac{15}{4} Q_1} \quad \overline{\frac{30}{4} Q_2}$$

It can be seen that the quantities of $Q_1$ and $Q_2$ produced are in the ratio of 1 : 2 and the means of production are also in the ratio of 1 : 2. Further, the rate of surplus of $Q_1 = Q_2 = 33.33$ percent.

It can be seen that the standard system is a special case where the ratio of value of Net Product to the value of means of production *i.e.* $\frac{P(I-A)Q}{PAQ}$ = Constant, at all levels of the rate of profit. This is because the Standard System is such that the Net Product and means of production are in the same proportions. Therefore value of the Net Product by value of means of production $\frac{P(I-A)Q}{PAQ}$ is independent of prices. When r changes, relative prices change, but the change in the relative prices will not affect the ratio $R = \frac{P(I-A)Q}{PAQ}$.

Consider the net product of the standard system of the example, which $5Q_1 - \frac{15}{4}Q_1$ and $10Q_2 - \frac{30}{4}Q_2$ or $\frac{5Q_1}{4}, \frac{10Q_2}{4}$. The means of production in the example are $\frac{15}{4}Q_1, \frac{30}{4}Q_2$.

$$\therefore R = \frac{\text{Net Product}}{\text{Means of Production}} = \frac{\left(\frac{5Q_1}{4}, \frac{10Q_2}{4}\right)}{\left(\frac{15Q_1}{4}, \frac{30Q_2}{4}\right)}$$

If $P_1 = 2;\ P_2 = 3;\ R = \dfrac{\frac{5}{4} \times 2 + \frac{10}{4} \times 3}{\frac{15}{4} \times 2 + \frac{30}{4} \times 3}$

$$= \frac{40}{4} \times \frac{4}{120} = \frac{4}{12}$$

$$= \tfrac{1}{3} = 33.3\%$$

If $P_1 = 2;\ P_2 = 4;\ R = \dfrac{\frac{5}{4} \times 2 + \frac{10}{4} \times 4}{\frac{15}{4} \times 2 + \frac{30}{4} \times 4}$

$$= \frac{25}{2} \times \frac{2}{75}$$

$$= \tfrac{1}{3} = 33.3\%$$

∴ The value of Net Product to value of means of production, in the Standard System, is unaffected by changes in relative prices in response to notional changes in rate of profit r. Hence in the Standard System,

$$R = \frac{P\,(I-A)\,Q}{PAQ} \text{ ......III for all r}$$

where, $0 \leqslant r \leqslant R$

Also $$r = \frac{(1-w)\,P\,(I-A)\,Q}{PAQ} \text{...... IV}$$

As in the Sraffa System surplus is shared by wage earners and profit earners. If the Net product is unity and wage rate is w, $1-w$=profit per man. From III & IV it follows that $r = (1-w)\,R$. Hence, the linear relation* between r and w.

---

*NOTE : Prof. G. Mathur Demonstrates(*) that the value free relation between rate of profit and the wage rate obtained by Sraffa is in the nature of an identity which emerges as a result of the assumptions made. Namely, that wage is paid post factum as a share of the net product, the surplus is entirely consumed and there is no consumption in advance of production and the net product or National Income is unity.

For, the equation $r = R\,(1-w)$ can be re-written as

$$\frac{r}{R} = 1-w \text{ or, } \frac{P}{K} \Big/ \frac{\text{Surplus}}{k} = 1-w, \quad \frac{P}{\text{Surplus}} = 1-w$$

Where, P is profit which is paid to the entrepreneurs after wage has been deducted from the net product.

(*) See G. Mathur : "The Capital Theory Base of Devt. Economics : Editional Observations", *World Development*, (Vol. 7, No. 10, Oct. 1979), pp. 901-922.

The linear relation which holds for the actual economy in value terms, with the proviso that the wage is in terms of the standard commodity, is considered to be of great significance in economic theory.[16] In fact it is said that "after a century and a half, Sraffa's standard commodity has thus fulfilled Ricardo's dream of an 'Invariable measure' of value".[17]

The linear relation is said to be highly significant, as it demonstrates an isolation of the value aspect from the distribution phenomenon. In other words, the distribution of income is seen to be independent of changes in relative prices. Further, the emergence of the linear relation is not dependant on pure labour theory of value, for Sraffa demonstrates that relative prices change in general in response to changes in distribution but the change in relative prices do not have an impact on either the rate of profit or on the Standard Ratio, R. Thus, even if pure labour values do not rule in a system, due to differences in organic composition of capital between processes, the distribution of income can be rendered free of changes in relative prices.

As mentioned earlier, Sraffa's analysis of determination of relative prices, including the complicated case of price reversals within a technique as a result of unidirectional change of rates of profit is within a static frame, where continuous expansion of goods overtime is absent, due to the assumption of the surplus of the system being completely consumed. Thus, Sraffa deliberately confines his analysis to the value aspect of Capital Theory, as he is in search of an invarient measure of value to solve the Ricardian Puzzle.

However, the extension of the Sraffa System to include growth is logically easy, since his system is one where the surplus over means of production, exists. If steady expansion of goods is visualised, the assumption of constant returns to scale, which Sraffa avoided becomes necessary, further, the propensity to consume of those who share the surplus must be less than unity. Steady expansion of the system is possible if it is assumed that wage earners consume the entire wage paid out of surplus while profit-earners propensity to consume is less than unity. Alternatively, it could also be assumed that both wage earners propensity to consume out of their share of the surplus and the propensity to consume of the profit earners are less than unity. In both cases, since steady expansion of goods overtime is being considered, production will have to be organised such that C-goods are produced to meet the consumption needs. This implies that the allocation will have to be biased in favour of C-good production. Hence the net product of the system cannot be in the same proportion as means of production, as C-goods will have to grow at a higher rate.

In case bonus wage is consumed entirely and profits are invested completely, the C-good will have to grow at a faster rate, but the vector of goods that constitute profits and means of production can still be in the same proportion. When profit earners also consume a part of their earnings, the goods that constitute profits cannot be in the same proportion as the means of production, in this case, the goods that form part of Investment (a vector, profits net of consumption) and means of production will be in the same proportions.

In case, it is assumed that wage is paid in terms of C-good in advance of production, the entire surplus accrues to the profit earners who do not consume out of it, and constant returns to scale prevails, the transformation of the Sraffa system to Von-Neumann Model of growth is complete.

Thus, with suitable changes in the assumptions, the Sraffa standard system can be extended to include steady expansion of goods. However, with the introduction of growth in the system, Sraffa's concept of the 'Standard Commodity' has only a limited use as an 'invarient measure' of value. For, whenever the wage rate changes, allocations change in general, giving rise to a different proportion of goods produced—a different standard system and with it a new 'Standard Commodity' would emerge.

Thus, constant proportion of the goods that form the Standard Commodity when growth is introduced to the system of production is possible only at a constant wage rate. Further, a change in the wage rate (paid in advance of production) changes the rate of surplus of the system, and therefore brings about changes in relative prices in general, even though technology is constant. Hence, it is not possible to isolate the impact of change in the wage rate, on the rate of profit from the simultaneous impact of change in relative prices on the rate of profit. The Standard system as well as the Standard Commodity become fluid concepts, once growth is introduced in the Sraffa System. The assumption of constant returns to scale helps only to a limited extent.

## REFERENCES

1. Luigi L. Pasinetti : *Lectures on the Theory of Production*, (Macmillan, 1978) pp. 71-119.
2. *Ibid.*, pp. 63-66.
3. *Ibid.*, pp. 75-76.
4. *Ibid.*, pp. 76-79.
5. P. Sraffa : *Production of Commodities by Means of Commodities, Prelude to a Critique of Economic Theory*, (Cambridge University Press, 1960), pp. 24-38.
6. *Ibid.*
7. *Ibid.*, p. 38.
8. G. Mathur : "On the Neutral Barton and Bartonesque Effect" (1973) Unpublished.
9. G. Mathur : *Planning for Steady Growth*, (Oxford University Press, 1965), pp. 159-162.
10. Not a Strictly Necessary Assumption.
11. For R = 4.09 technique A switches with a Neutral Wicksell Technology with the same order of mechanization. In other words Technology responds like a Neutral Wicksell Technology at R = 4.09. Therefore prices cross. See Appendix for the solutions.
12. NOTE : When the net product per worker is made equal to unity, the share of wages in the net product and the wage rate are equal. See : Luigi L. Pasinetti : *Lectures on the Theory of Production*, (Macmillan, 1978) p. 85.
13. *Ibid.*, pp. 115-116.
14. *Ibid.*, pp. 118-120.
15. *Ibid.*, p. 85.
16. *Ibid.*, pp. 114-116.
17. *Ibid.*, p. 120.

CHAPTER V

# On Switching and Reswitching

SRAFFA'S EXPOSITION of reswitching of techniques established without doubt that there is no reason to expect that a higher rate of profit be associated with a lower value of capital per man, in general. For, reswitching of techniques means that the same technique becomes optimum at two different rates of profit while being inoptimum for rates of profit in between. Therefore, once the possibility of reswitching of techniques is accepted it implies that a change in the rate of profit in a given direction can be associated with both a higher and a lower value of capital per man. Since this result negated the accepted inverse monotonic relationship between the rate of profit and capital per man, there was a tendency to look upon the possibility of reswitching as an odd occurrence which could be ignored.

For instance, Joan Robinson while discussing choice of techniques, examined the possibility of Reswitching of techniques much earlier than Sraffa[1] but thought it to be a "perverse" case. Champernowne was aware of the theoretical possibility earlier than Sraffa but chose to assume away Reswitching.[2]

It is not surprising therefore, that Lavahari decided to challenge Sraffa's results—results which cut at the roots of the neo-classical production function and related concepts. He tried to prove that while Reswitching may occur between methods of production of a single good, the phenomenon is ruled out for techniques of production which are indecomposable. In other words, if the Von Neumann assumption of every good entering the production of every other, directly or indirectly is made, once a technological matrix comprising of set of processes of production is rejected as inoptimum at a particular rate of profit, it cannot become optimum at any other higher rates of profit.

However Lavahari's attempt was abortive for Pasinetti's defence of Sraffa's reswitching of techniques was so effective that the controversy ended by Lavahari's admission that his non-switching theorem was false.

Pasinetti reformulated,[3] Sraffa's example in coefficient matrix form with a slight modification. In Sraffa's example the two techniques which produce different products "differ in three of their labour terms", the techniques are otherwise identical. In Pasinetti's example the two techniques differ in their labour requirements and in their distribution over time, but both techniques produce the same commodity G. Technology A requires .8 units of G in period zero and 20 units of labour 8 years earlier, to produce one unit of G. Technology B to produce the same one unit of G needs .8 units of G and 24 units of labour in period zero, in addition it requires one unit of labour 25 years earlier.

These two technologies are represented in a matrix notation by a "break up" of the production process of G into different activities, each activity corresponding to a year of the production process. Thus, technology A is represented by a 9 × 9 matrix A and vector of labour coefficients $l_a'$ while technology B is represented by a 26 × 26 matrix B and vector of labour inputs $l_b$ as follows :

$$A = \begin{matrix} .8 & 0 & 0 & 0 & 0 & 0 & 0 & 0 & 0 \\ 0 & 1 & 0 & 0 & 0 & 0 & 0 & 0 & 0 \\ 0 & 0 & 1 & 0 & 0 & 0 & 0 & 0 & 0 \\ 0 & 0 & 0 & 1 & 0 & 0 & 0 & 0 & 0 \\ 0 & 0 & 0 & 0 & 1 & 0 & 0 & 0 & 0 \\ 0 & 0 & 0 & 0 & 0 & 1 & 0 & 0 & 0 \\ 0 & 0 & 0 & 0 & 0 & 0 & 1 & 0 & 0 \\ 0 & 0 & 0 & 0 & 0 & 0 & 0 & 1 & 0 \\ 0 & 0 & 0 & 0 & 0 & 0 & 0 & 0 & 1 \end{matrix}$$

$$1_a = \quad [0\ 0\ 0\ 0\ 0\ 0\ 0\ 0\ 0\ 20]$$

$$B = \begin{matrix}
.8 & 0 & 0 & 0 & 0 & 0 & 0 & 0 & 0 & 0 & 0 & 0 & 0 & 0 & 0 & 0 & 0 & 0 & 0 & 0 & 0 & 0 & 0 & 0 & 0 & 0 \\
0 & 1 & 0 & 0 & 0 & 0 & 0 & 0 & 0 & 0 & 0 & 0 & 0 & 0 & 0 & 0 & 0 & 0 & 0 & 0 & 0 & 0 & 0 & 0 & 0 & 0 \\
0 & 0 & 1 & 0 & 0 & 0 & 0 & 0 & 0 & 0 & 0 & 0 & 0 & 0 & 0 & 0 & 0 & 0 & 0 & 0 & 0 & 0 & 0 & 0 & 0 & 0 \\
0 & 0 & 0 & 1 & 0 & 0 & 0 & 0 & 0 & 0 & 0 & 0 & 0 & 0 & 0 & 0 & 0 & 0 & 0 & 0 & 0 & 0 & 0 & 0 & 0 & 0 \\
0 & 0 & 0 & 0 & 1 & 0 & 0 & 0 & 0 & 0 & 0 & 0 & 0 & 0 & 0 & 0 & 0 & 0 & 0 & 0 & 0 & 0 & 0 & 0 & 0 & 0 \\
0 & 0 & 0 & 0 & 0 & 1 & 0 & 0 & 0 & 0 & 0 & 0 & 0 & 0 & 0 & 0 & 0 & 0 & 0 & 0 & 0 & 0 & 0 & 0 & 0 & 0 \\
0 & 0 & 0 & 0 & 0 & 0 & 1 & 0 & 0 & 0 & 0 & 0 & 0 & 0 & 0 & 0 & 0 & 0 & 0 & 0 & 0 & 0 & 0 & 0 & 0 & 0 \\
0 & 0 & 0 & 0 & 0 & 0 & 0 & 1 & 0 & 0 & 0 & 0 & 0 & 0 & 0 & 0 & 0 & 0 & 0 & 0 & 0 & 0 & 0 & 0 & 0 & 0 \\
0 & 0 & 0 & 0 & 0 & 0 & 0 & 0 & 1 & 0 & 0 & 0 & 0 & 0 & 0 & 0 & 0 & 0 & 0 & 0 & 0 & 0 & 0 & 0 & 0 & 0 \\
0 & 0 & 0 & 0 & 0 & 0 & 0 & 0 & 0 & 1 & 0 & 0 & 0 & 0 & 0 & 0 & 0 & 0 & 0 & 0 & 0 & 0 & 0 & 0 & 0 & 0 \\
0 & 0 & 0 & 0 & 0 & 0 & 0 & 0 & 0 & 0 & 1 & 0 & 0 & 0 & 0 & 0 & 0 & 0 & 0 & 0 & 0 & 0 & 0 & 0 & 0 & 0 \\
0 & 0 & 0 & 0 & 0 & 0 & 0 & 0 & 0 & 0 & 0 & 1 & 0 & 0 & 0 & 0 & 0 & 0 & 0 & 0 & 0 & 0 & 0 & 0 & 0 & 0 \\
0 & 0 & 0 & 0 & 0 & 0 & 0 & 0 & 0 & 0 & 0 & 0 & 1 & 0 & 0 & 0 & 0 & 0 & 0 & 0 & 0 & 0 & 0 & 0 & 0 & 0 \\
0 & 0 & 0 & 0 & 0 & 0 & 0 & 0 & 0 & 0 & 0 & 0 & 0 & 1 & 0 & 0 & 0 & 0 & 0 & 0 & 0 & 0 & 0 & 0 & 0 & 0 \\
0 & 0 & 0 & 0 & 0 & 0 & 0 & 0 & 0 & 0 & 0 & 0 & 0 & 0 & 1 & 0 & 0 & 0 & 0 & 0 & 0 & 0 & 0 & 0 & 0 & 0 \\
0 & 0 & 0 & 0 & 0 & 0 & 0 & 0 & 0 & 0 & 0 & 0 & 0 & 0 & 0 & 1 & 0 & 0 & 0 & 0 & 0 & 0 & 0 & 0 & 0 & 0 \\
0 & 0 & 0 & 0 & 0 & 0 & 0 & 0 & 0 & 0 & 0 & 0 & 0 & 0 & 0 & 0 & 1 & 0 & 0 & 0 & 0 & 0 & 0 & 0 & 0 & 0 \\
0 & 0 & 0 & 0 & 0 & 0 & 0 & 0 & 0 & 0 & 0 & 0 & 0 & 0 & 0 & 0 & 0 & 1 & 0 & 0 & 0 & 0 & 0 & 0 & 0 & 0 \\
0 & 0 & 0 & 0 & 0 & 0 & 0 & 0 & 0 & 0 & 0 & 0 & 0 & 0 & 0 & 0 & 0 & 0 & 1 & 0 & 0 & 0 & 0 & 0 & 0 & 0 \\
0 & 0 & 0 & 0 & 0 & 0 & 0 & 0 & 0 & 0 & 0 & 0 & 0 & 0 & 0 & 0 & 0 & 0 & 0 & 1 & 0 & 0 & 0 & 0 & 0 & 0 \\
0 & 0 & 0 & 0 & 0 & 0 & 0 & 0 & 0 & 0 & 0 & 0 & 0 & 0 & 0 & 0 & 0 & 0 & 0 & 0 & 1 & 0 & 0 & 0 & 0 & 0 \\
0 & 0 & 0 & 0 & 0 & 0 & 0 & 0 & 0 & 0 & 0 & 0 & 0 & 0 & 0 & 0 & 0 & 0 & 0 & 0 & 0 & 1 & 0 & 0 & 0 & 0 \\
0 & 0 & 0 & 0 & 0 & 0 & 0 & 0 & 0 & 0 & 0 & 0 & 0 & 0 & 0 & 0 & 0 & 0 & 0 & 0 & 0 & 0 & 1 & 0 & 0 & 0 \\
0 & 0 & 0 & 0 & 0 & 0 & 0 & 0 & 0 & 0 & 0 & 0 & 0 & 0 & 0 & 0 & 0 & 0 & 0 & 0 & 0 & 0 & 0 & 1 & 0 & 0 \\
0 & 0 & 0 & 0 & 0 & 0 & 0 & 0 & 0 & 0 & 0 & 0 & 0 & 0 & 0 & 0 & 0 & 0 & 0 & 0 & 0 & 0 & 0 & 0 & 1 & 0 \\
0 & 0 & 0 & 0 & 0 & 0 & 0 & 0 & 0 & 0 & 0 & 0 & 0 & 0 & 0 & 0 & 0 & 0 & 0 & 0 & 0 & 0 & 0 & 0 & 0 & 1
\end{matrix}$$

$$1_b = 24\ 0\ 0\ 0\ 0\ 0\ 0\ 0\ 0\ 0\ 0\ 0\ 0\ 0\ 0\ 0\ 0\ 0\ 0\ 0\ 0\ 0\ 0\ 0\ 0\ 1$$

The technologies can also be represented as,

$(A) = (a_{ij})$ when $i \neq j$, $a_{ij} = 0$

when $i = j = 1$, $a_{ij} = .8$ and

when $i = j = 1, 2......9$ $a_{ij} = 1$

and $1_a = [\,0\ 0\ 0\ 0\ 0\ 0\ 0\ 0\ 0\ 20]$

$(B) = (b_{ij})$ when $i \neq j$, $b_{ij} = 0$

when $i = j = 1$, $b_{ij} = .8$ and

when $i = j = 2, 3,......26$ $b_{ij} = 1$

and $l_b = [24\ 000000000000000000000001]$

The technology matrices can also be represented in a simple form as follows :

$$(A) = \begin{bmatrix} .8 & 0 \\ 0 & X_1 \end{bmatrix}$$ Where $X_1$ is a unit matrix of order eight

$$(B) = \begin{bmatrix} .8 & 0 \\ 8 & X_2 \end{bmatrix}$$ Where $X_2$ is a unit matrix of order twenty five

For the two technologies a and b and relative prices can be worked out by solving the set of simultaneous equations derived from the matrices, using the condition of equilibrium that the same rate of profit rules amongst different processes within each technique. In this case the different processes of the technique are assumed to coexist in time.

Pasinetti derives the equation which connects the wage rate and the rate of profit corresponding to technique a as,

$$W_a = \frac{P_a(0)\,[1-.8\,(1+r)]}{20\,(1+r)^8} \qquad \ldots\ldots (1)$$

Where $P_a$ (o), the price of G is taken as the numeraire of the system. The w-r curve represented by the equation (1) implies that different processes of production of the technique exist over time. In other words capital is being viewed from the lengthwise section like the Austrian Capital Theorists.

Equation (1) can be rewritten as :

$$W_a\,20\,(1+r)^8 + P_a(o)\ .8\,(1+r) = P_a(o)$$

*i.e.*, wage cost compounded to the present plus value of raw material input compounded to the present equals the value of the final product. While the equation expresses the general value theory, the particular example is applicable only to very simple cases of production, for the time structure stands for total time taken in years to produce Gthrough barehand process, *i.e.*, he assumes that fixed capital is not required for both technologies.

Similarly he derives the w-r curve for technology b as,

$$W_b = P_b\,(o)\,\frac{[1-0.8\,(1+r)]}{24\,(1+r)^{25}} \qquad \ldots\ldots (2)$$

The curves that these two technologies trace for different wage rates (or rates of profit) can be worked out by finding the values of r for different w or *vice versa* from equations. (1) and (2). Pasinetti has shown that when r takes values from 1 to 25 the curves traced by the two techniques are as in fig. (1). The curves intersect at r = 3.6 percent, 16.2 percent and at 25 percent. Hence, for interest rates 0 to 3.6, technology a is to be preferred, since, it gives a higher wage rate for the same rate of profit compared to technique b, in the range 3.6 percent $<r<$ 16.2 percent technique b will be preferred and in the range 16.2 percent $<r<$25 percent technology a will be preferred once again. The numerical examples therefore confirm the theoretical possibility of reswitching (See figure 1).

It can be observed that in Pasinetti's examples, the inputs of labour and commodity G are needed at the beginning of the process of production and in the final period. In between, the intermediate goods change their form without the assistance of even labour. Further, following Sraffa, he accounts wages post factum out of the surplus and assumes explicitly, that fixed capital is not used. His examples are, therefore, remote from reality when interpreted in the context of modern technological structure of production. Since time structure of production stands for total time taken in years to produce G and the intermediate goods do not require any input, his examples can represent planting of trees or production of wine, where mere passage of time enhances the value of a good.

However, Pasinetti's examples, though simple in form successfully illustrate the cause of reswitching as the difference in organic composition of capital between processes within a technique and between techniques. In his examples, uneven distribution of labour input and commodity G over time is the cause of reswitching of techniques. His numerical examples and the discussion on reswitching led Lavahari to accept that his non-switching theorem was false, although Pasinetti's examples were not indecomposable technologies.

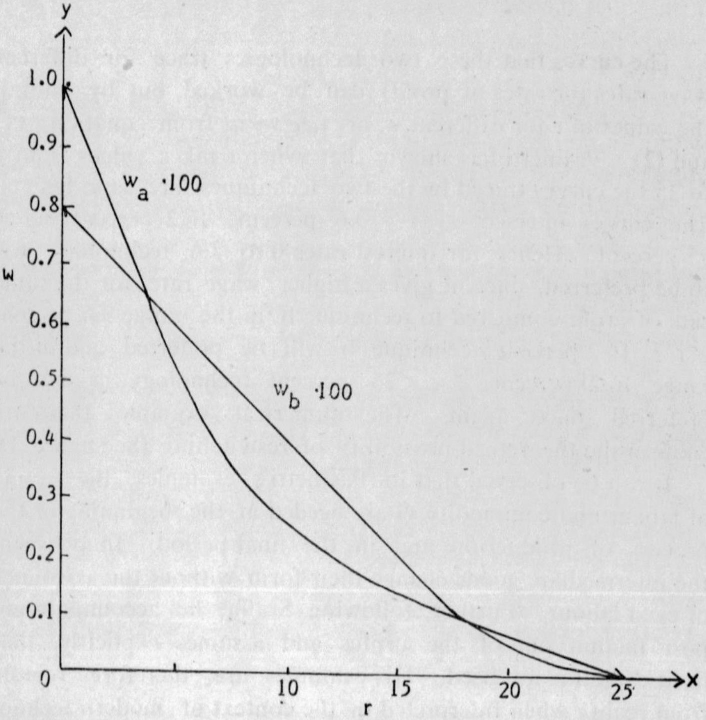


Fig. (1)

Subsequently, Bruno Burmeister and Sheshinski[4] proved that even when the technologies are indecomposable the recurrence of "a whole matrix of activities or a technique of production" at different rates of profit is possible. Thus, Sraffa's results were accepted and reswitching of techniques is no longer considered as an odd or "perverse" case in capital theory.

While analysing the conditions for switching of technologies it has been established, that in general, an n-capital goods model can have n switches with another n capital goods model. The proof rests on the fact that, if the w-r equations are derived for the two techniques and if the condition of equal wage rates at the switch points is used, an $n^{th}$ degree polynomial in r emerges from the two w-r curves. Since, an $n^{th}$ degree equation in r must necessarily have n roots, it is established that the two techniques can cross their paths n times, which implies that the same technique can "come back" n−1 times.

Given any technique of production, either with only circulating capital as input like the Pasinetti examples, or using durable or depreciation of fixed capital, one can derive the corresponding w-r relationship, conventionally called the factor price frontier. Once the w-r equation is derived by plugging in values of w (or r), the values of r (or w) can be obtained and when these are plotted on a two dimensional plane, we get the curve (path) traced out by each technique, as distribution changes. In general, the wage rate of profit curve can be a straight line, a curve convex or concave to the origin and can also be convex for certain values of r and concave thereafter (or *vice versa*), the w-r curve, however, must necessarily be downward slopping. Thus, w-r curves can take the following shapes. See figures 2 to 9.

The w-r curve can change its convexity as in figure (9) more than once. The conditions for it to change its convexity will be discussed in detail later in this chapter.

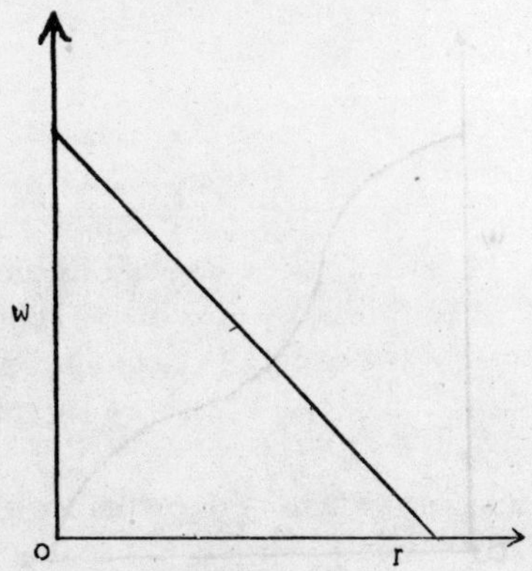


Fig. (2)

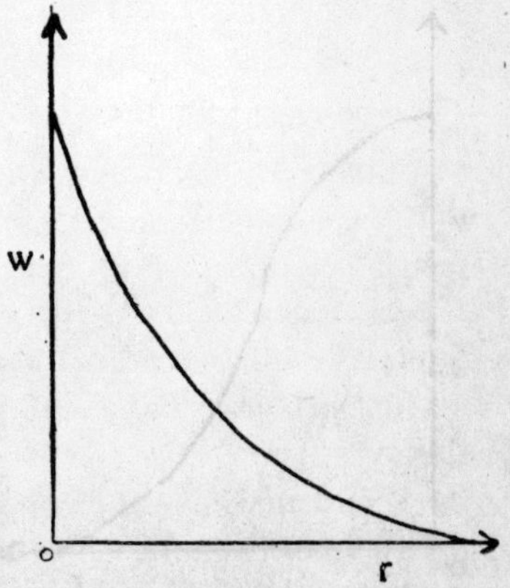


Fig. (3)

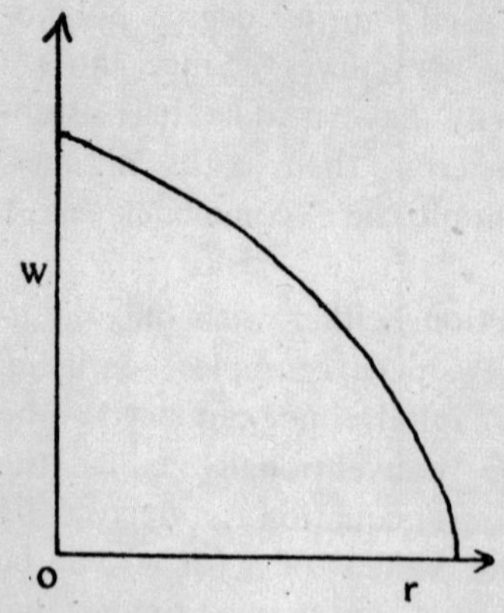


Fig. (4)

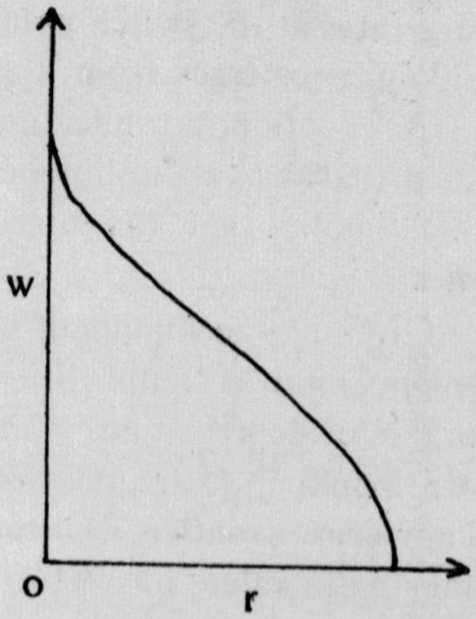


Fig. (5)

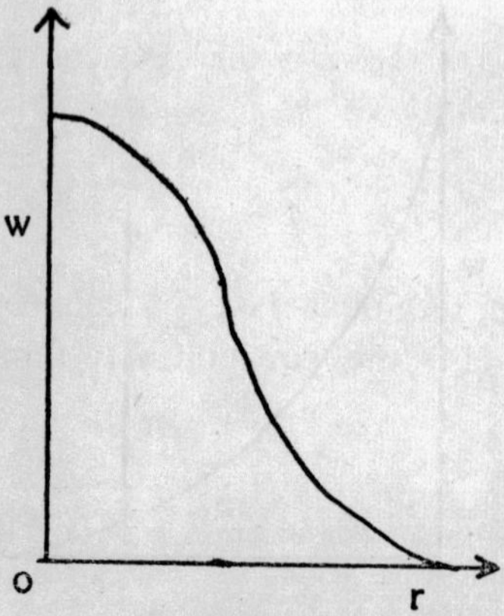


Fig. (6)

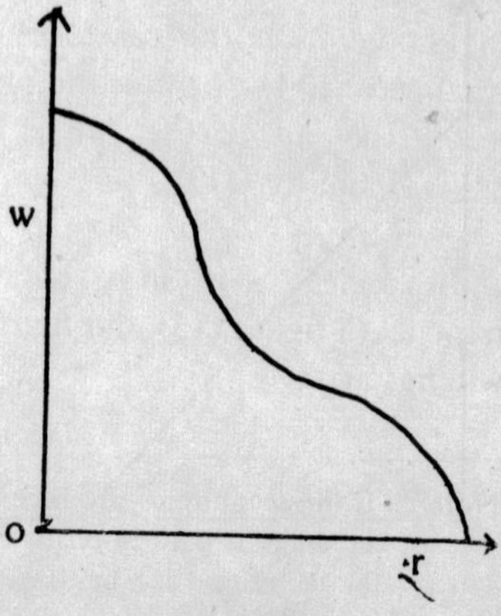


Fig. (7)

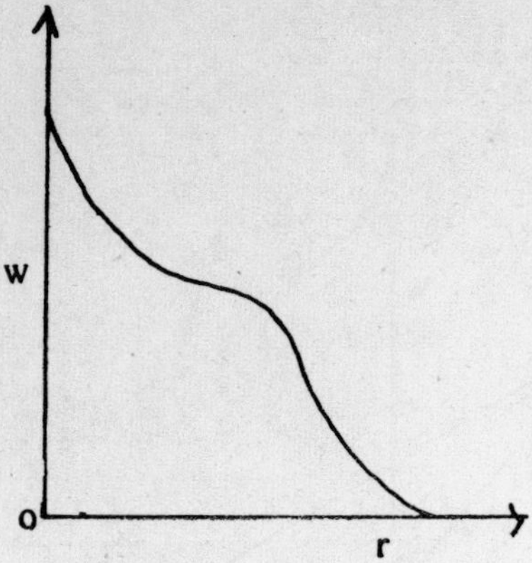


Fig. (8)

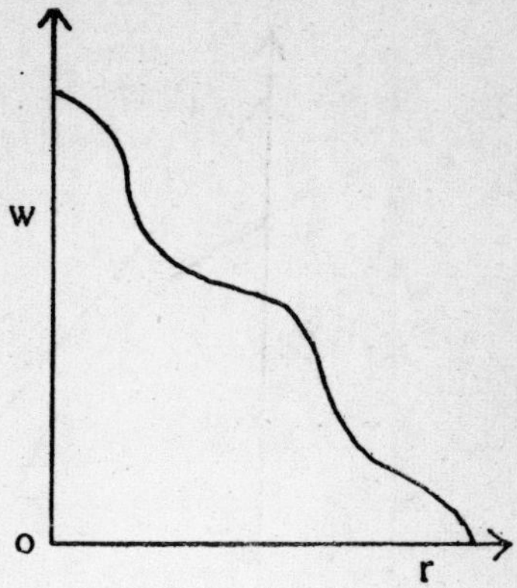


Fig. (9)

When the w-r curve of one technique is intersected by the w-r curve of another, a switch point occurs. A switch point is a point of indifference as regards the choice between the two techniques, for at the switch point, both techniques give the same rate of profit and wage rate. It follows for all other rates of profit, one technique is to be preferred to the other, for it will yield a higher wage rate for given r or *vice versa*.

In case, two techniques* have a straight line as their w-r curves, it is obvious that at best there can be only one switch point between them, as the figure (10) indicates. No reswitching is possible in this case. If one of the w-r curves is convex or concave to the origin, the possibility of two switches arise even if the path of the other technique is straight line. See fig. (11) and fig. (12).

In case the w-r curve of one technique takes a complex shape as in figure (13) and figure (14) the possibilities of three switches arise.

---

*Note :—If the techniques produce the same consumption good and if the wage is paid in terms of this wage good, the w-r curves of the technique can be drawn on the same diagram.

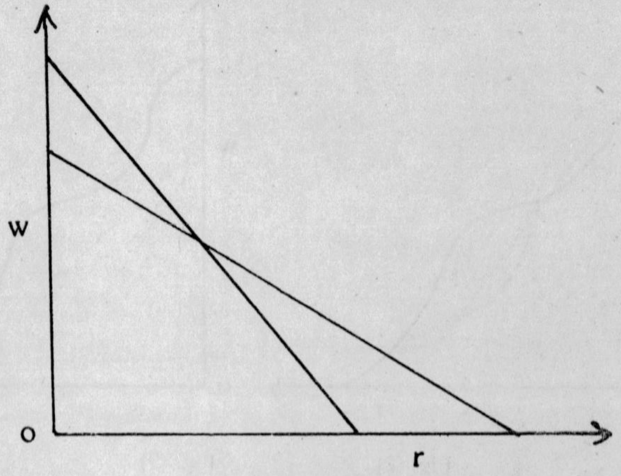


Fig. (10)

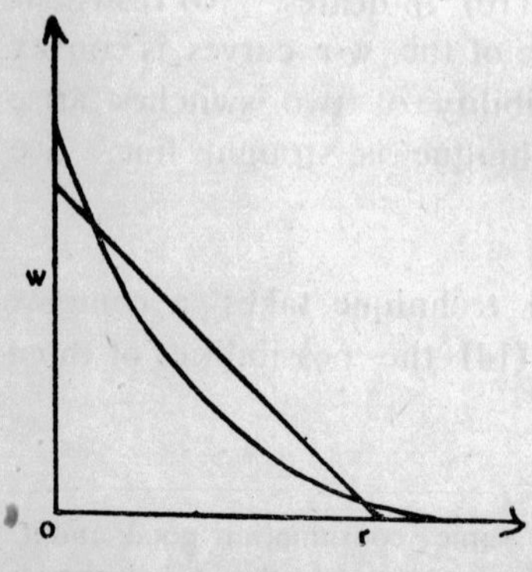


Fig. (11)

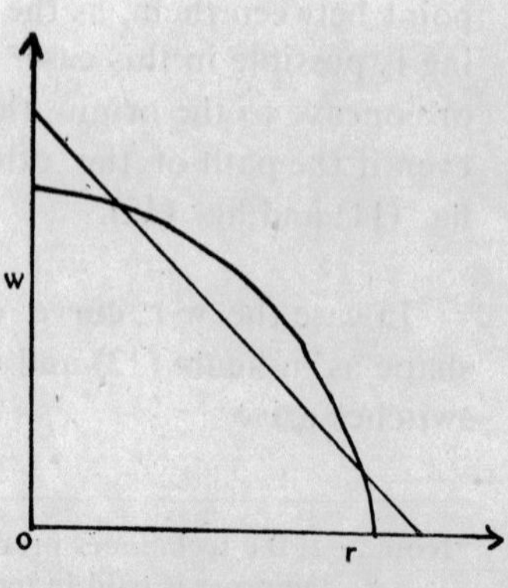


Fig. (12)

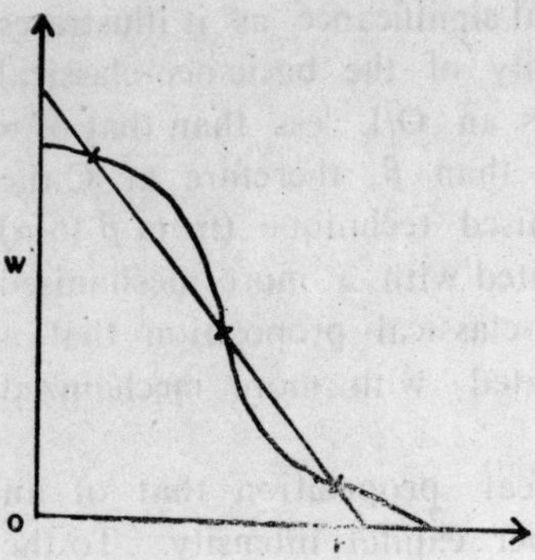


Fig. (13)

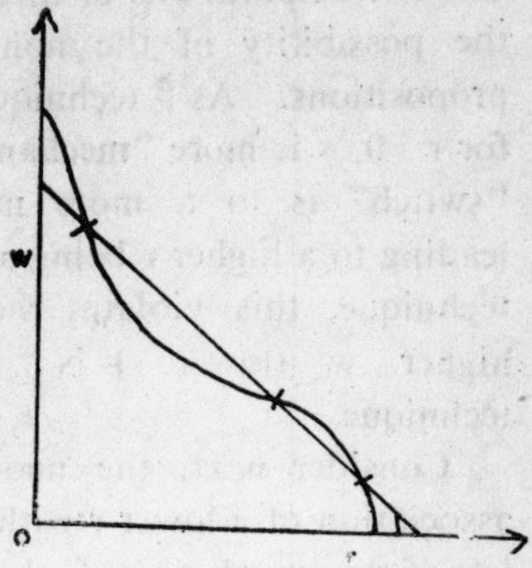


Fig. (14)

If two techniques $\alpha$ and $\beta$ have their w-r curves as in the figure (12), reswitching of techniques takes place at the switch point c. The "factor price frontier" in this case would be ab along $\alpha$, bc along $\beta$ and cd along $\alpha$ once again (reswitching).

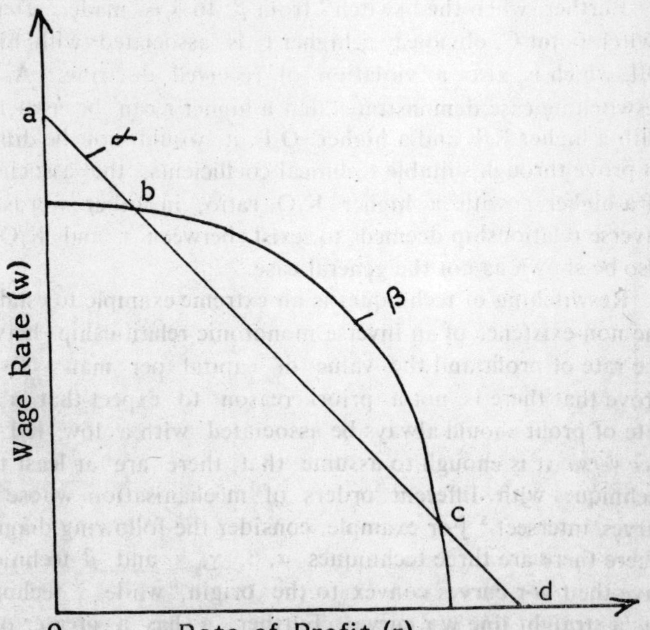


Fig. (12)

The switch point c is of theoretical significance as it illustrates the possibility of the non-validity of the basic neo-classical propositions. As β technique has an O/L less than that of α for r=0, α is more "mechanised" than β, therefore at C the "switch" is to a more mechanised technique (from β to α) leading to a higher r being associated with a more mechanised technique, this violates the neo-classical proposition that a higher w (lower r) is associated with more mechanized technique.

Consider next, the neo-classical proposition that of an association of a lower r with higher capital intensity. To the left of the switch point C the value of K/L of β technique is less than the value of K/L of α tenhnique or else β could not have dominated as its O/L is lower than of α. Therefore, to the right of C when the switch has been made to α, we would get an association of a higher r with higher K/L (termed as capital reversing) negating the traditional inverse monotonic relationship between r and K/L.

Further, when the "switch" from β to α is made, after the switch point C, obviously a higher r is associated with higher O/L which is also a violation of received doctrine. As the reswitching case demonstrates that a higher r can be associated with a higher K/L and a higher O/L, it would not be difficult to prove through suitable technical coefficients, the association of a higher r with a higher K/O ratio, in other words the inverse relationship deemed to exist between r and K/O can also be shown as not the general case.

Reswitching of techniques is an extreme example to establish the non-existence of an inverse monotonic relationship between the rate of profit and the value of capital per man. To disprove that there is, not a priori reason to expect that a high rate of profit should always be associated with a low K/L and *vice versa*, it is enough to assume that there are at least three techniques with different orders of mechanisation whose w-r curves intersect.[5] For example, consider the following diagram, where there are three techniques α, β, γ. α and β techniques have their w-r curves convex to the origin, while γ technique has a straight line w-r curve. Further, α has a greater order of mechanisation than $\beta$ and $\beta$ in turn belongs to a higher order of mechanisation than.

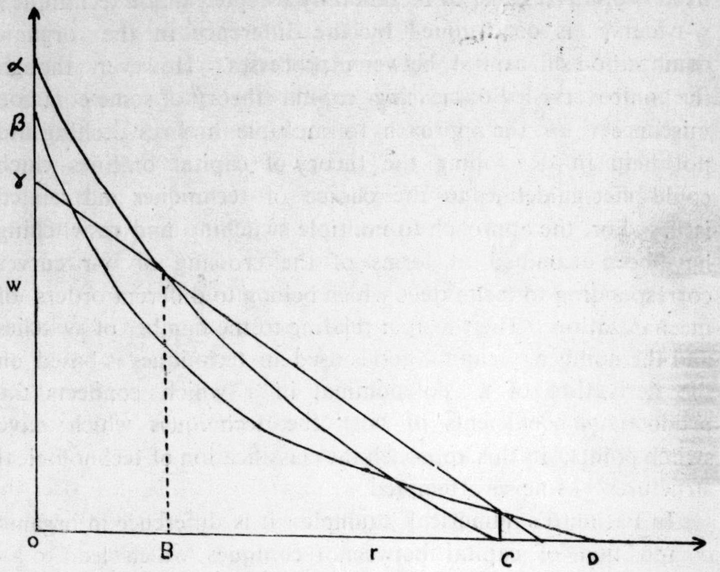


Fig. (15)

From the diagram it can be seen that for $O<\gamma<OB$, $\alpha$ technique is optimum, for $OB< r < BC$, $\gamma$ takes over, since $\gamma$ has a lower order of mechanization, at $r = OB$ for $\gamma$ to emerge as optimum the value of K/L must be lower than that of $\alpha$, hence as $r \uparrow$ $K/L \downarrow$, the switch at OB is in conformity with traditional capital theory. However, for $r = CD$, $\beta$ dominates over $\gamma$, in the BC range of r, $\gamma$ is to be preferred, since $\gamma$ has a lower O/L than $\beta$ it implies that $\gamma$'s K/L is much lower than $\beta$ in the range BC and therefore, it is obvious that in the CD range the switch is in favour of a higher K/L in response to a higher r. As r rises from O to D the value of K/L is lower, then higher. Thus, at the second switch point the inverse monotonic relationship between r and K/L is violated.

Thus, the controversy which was sparked off by Sraffa's Book[6] led to a re-examination of classical and neo-classical capital theory. Incidently it was proved that reswitching of techniques are possible for decomposable as well as for indecomposable technologies with and without explicit use of fixed capital. It came to be generally accepted that a technique's w-r curve is conditioned by the difference in the organic composition of capital between processes. However, though the controversy led to clearing capital theory of some common misconceptions, the approach to multiple and reswitching did not help in developing the theory of capital on lines which could offer guidelines to the choice of techniques and related issues. For, the approach to multiple switching and reswitching have been examined in terms of the crossing of w-r curves corresponding to techniques which belong to different orders of mechanization. The theorem relating to the number of switches and the number of capital goods used in techniques is based on the derivation of a polynominal in r which connects the productivity coefficients of both the techniques which have switch points. In this approach the classification of technological structures was never attempted.

In Pasinetti's numerical examples, it is difference in organic composition of capital between techniques which lead to an intersection of their w-r curves. The different processes within the two techniques have labour and commodity G distributed differently over time, where the time structure itself is viewed as total time taken in years to produce the commodity G. In other words, the different processes which compose the technique exist in different years. While it is true that the w-r curve of any technique is conditioned by the change in relative prices of the different commodities produced in different processes, this approach cannot give insight into the relationship between technological structure and the nature of the w-r curve. For, organic composition can differ between processes, due to difference in wage rates, value of raw material inputs or due to the difference in the value of fixed capital or a combination of any of these two or all three. In this approach it is not possible to isolate the role of the various components that influence the organic composition of capital. Therefore, the classification of techniques in terms of their technological structure could not be attempted.

In the works of Gautam Mathur, we find for the first time, an attempt to classify different technological structures in terms of productivities. Following Sraffa and Neumann models, a technique is viewed in his system, as a set of processes which are self-sufficient except for natural resources and labour. Fixed capital of different types enter as inputs in different processes and they emerge as joint products of the system. Wages are paid in advance of production in terms of bags of corn, which is also the numeraire of the prices.

In simple Sraffa-Neumann Models[7] the assumption of everlasting capital goods and production of a single consumption good is made, though the model can take care of depreciating capital goods, more than one raw material input and multiple consumption goods.

The classification of technological structure has been made with the help of the assumption of uniform wage rates in processes within a technique. The assumption of uniform wage makes it possible to highlight the role of productivities of the technological structure in conditioning the shape of the w-r curve, corresponding to a technique. In other words the role of productivities in influencing the nature and shape of the w-r curve is brought out. In this approach, it is possible to classify techniques as positive, reverse and Neutral Wicksell technologies in terms of the ordering of the productivities of the man equipment team in the investment sector. For example, the simple one capital good case in Sraffa-Neumann Model with the following assumptions ; (1) Wages are paid in advance of production in terms of the consumption good corn ; (2) Workers do not save out of their wages, they do not get a share out of the surplus ; (3) The capital good does not depreciate ; (4) The technology is such that there are only two processes of production, one process for the production of C-good corn and the other process produces the durable equipment e. Equipment e produces with the aid of labour more of its kind and the C-good. If the output per man equipment team in corn making process is 6 (bags of corn) and in equipment e making process, it is 1 (physical equipment), the technique A is depicted as follows :

TECHNIQUE A

| Men | C | e | | C | e |
|---|---|---|---|---|---|
| 1 | 1 | 1 | ⟶ | 6 | 1 |
| 1 | 1 | 1 | ⟶ | 0 | 1 + 1 |

The price equations can be derived from technique A as,

$$(1 + P) \ R = 6 + P \quad \text{———} \quad (1)$$

$$(1 + P) \ R = 2P \quad \text{———} \quad (2)$$

Where, P is the price of the equipment e in terms of corn and R is the coefficient of profit assumed to be the same in both processes of production.

Solving for P we get, $\dfrac{(1 + P) R}{(1 + P) R} = \dfrac{6 + P}{2P}$ ...... (3)

or $P = 6$

From equation (3) it can be seen that P is independent of the wage rate, in other words the value of P in relation to the C-good is not affected by the change in wage rate as long as the wage is uniform between the two processes of the technique A. A technological matrix which is such that, at uniform wage rate among its processes, gives a set of relative prices which are unaffected by changes in distribution has been termed as Neutral Wicksell Technology.[8] In this system, two sector models at uniform wage, belong to Neutral Wicksell category.

If a technique has one more department in the investment sector even at uniform wage, the technology can exhibit non-Neutral Wicksell response, *i.e.*, the relative prices can change when distribution changes. The price of the equipment can be higher at a higher wage rate, termed as Positive Wicksell Effect, or the price of the equipment can be lower for a higher wage rate termed as Negative or Reverse Wicksell Effect.[9] When wage rate is kept uniform, Wicksell effect arises due to ordering of productivities when techniques are a set of processes depicted in an input-output matrix form. In this case, the Positive or Reverse Wicksell Effect owes its origin to the difference in productivity coefficients per man equipment team between different processes within a technique of production. Thus, in Sraffa-Neumann model, technology B, with ascending productivity coefficients per man equipment team in the investment sectors would show positive Wicksell[10] response, while technology C with descending productivity coefficients will be subject to Reverse Wicksell response.

TECHNOLOGY MATRIX B

| Men | C | $e_1$ | $e_2$ | | C | $e_1$ | $e_2$ |
|---|---|---|---|---|---|---|---|
| 1 | 1 | 1 | 0 | ⟶ | 10 | 1 | 0 |
| 1 | 1 | 0 | 1 | ⟶ | 0 | 2 | 1 |
| 1 | 1 | 0 | 1 | ⟶ | 0 | 0 | 3 + 1 |

TECHNOLOGY MATRIX C

| Men | C | $E_1$ | $E_2$ | | C | $E_1$ | $E_2$ |
|---|---|---|---|---|---|---|---|
| 1 | 1 | 1 | 0 | ⟶ | 10 | 1 | 0 |
| 1 | 1 | 0 | 1 | ⟶ | 0 | 2 | 1 |
| 1 | 1 | 0 | 1 | ⟶ | 0 | 0 | 1 + 1 |

In other words in technique C, $e_2$ will be less expensive in terms of corn, the numeraire, as higher wage levels are considered. In contrast, in technique B as higher wage levels are considered the value of $E_2$ in terms of corn will be higher.

In case the productivity coefficients in the investment sector is neither in ascending or descending order, but are constant as in technology matrix D, we get the simple (special) case of the relative price of equipment constant and independent of wage rates (or rates of profit).

TECHNOLOGY MATRIX D

| Men | C | e'1 | e'2 | | C | e'1 | e'2 |
|---|---|---|---|---|---|---|---|
| 1 | 1 | 1 | 0 | ⟶ | 4 | 1 | 0 |
| 1 | 1 | 0 | 1 | ⟶ | 0 | 2 | 1 |
| 1 | 1 | 0 | 1 | ⟶ | 0 | 0 | 2+1 |

By eliminating differences in the wage rates which could be a cause for a difference in organic composition of capital, the role played by Technical Coefficients of production, in causing difference in organic composition and thus leading to change in structure of relative prices in response to change in distribution is highlighted in Sraffa-Neumann Model. Thus, this approach allows classification of Techniques in terms of Wicksell Responses through the ordering of productivity coefficients.

In this system, the two capital goods model can demonstrate three different types of Wicksell Effects, depending upon the ordering of the productivities of man equipment team in capital goods producing processes.

When the number of departments in the investment sector is three in a technique, the technological matrix can exhibit all the pure cases of Wicksell Effects discussed so far, in addition, it can also be a combination of different Wicksell Effects *i.e.* the relative prices can change as if the technological structure is pure Positive Wicksell type for some ranges of the wage rates and the response of relative prices can conform to Reverse Wicksell structure at some other ranges of the wage rates. Thus, the price of the highest order good can be higher in terms of the C-good as numeraire, for some ranges of the wage rates and can be lower for still higher ranges of the wage rates, within a given technique of production.

In the Sraffa-Neumann model the price of the capital good (highest order) is connected to the rate of interest (equal to the rate of profit) by the Fundamental Equation[11] for the Self-Reproducing Durable Capital Case as,

$$P_n = \frac{b_o b \ldots\ldots b_{n-1}}{b_1 b_2 \ldots b_n - [i\, b_2 b_3 \ldots b_{n-1}(b_1 - b_n) + i^2\, b_3 b_4 \ldots b_{n-1}(b_2 - b_n) + \ldots i^{n-1}(b_{n-1} - b_n)]}$$

where 'bs' are the technical output entries of the n + 1 process, 'is' the rate of interest and $P_n$, the price of the highest order capital good expressed in terms of the consumption good. When the above equation for the n capital goods model is reduced to 3 capital goods model, the equation will be,

$$P_3 = \frac{b_o\, b_1\, b_2}{b_1\, b_2\, b_3 - [i\, b_2\, (b_1 - b_3) + i^2\, (b_2 - b_3)]}$$

For any given technique 'bs' are constants, therefore, the equation can be written as,

$$P_3 = \frac{C_o}{C_1 - [i\, b_2\, (\triangle_1) + i^2\, (\triangle_2)]}$$

Where $C_o$ and $C_1$ are constants and,

$$\triangle_1 = (b_1 - b_3),\ \triangle_2 = (b_2 - b_3)$$

If $\phi\,(i) = i\, b_2\, \triangle_1 + i^2\, \triangle_3$, Wicksell Effects can be defined[12] with the help of $\phi$ (i).

*Case I* : If $\phi$ (i) is positive and i is lower (*i.e.* w is higher) $P_n$ is lower. In other words, If $\triangle_1 > 0$ and $\triangle_3 > 0$, $\phi$ (i) will be positive, in this case if i is lower $P_n$ is lower, i lower implies w higher as the technique of production is constant. Hence, w ↑ $P_n$ ↓ which has been termed as Reverse Wicksell

Effect. It must be noted that $\triangle_1 > 0$ implies $b_1 > b_3$ and $\triangle_2 > 0$, $b_2 > b_3$ *i.e.* the productivity coefficients are in descending order.

*Case II* : If $\phi$ (i) is negative and i is lower $P_n$ is higher, *i.e.* i lower means w higher, w higher $P_n$ higher has been termed as positive Wicksell Effect. For $\phi$ (i) to be negative either $\triangle_1 < 0$ and $\triangle_2 < 0$ or $\triangle_1 < 0$ and $\triangle_2 > 0$ but $| \triangle_1 | > | \triangle_2 |$. In case $\triangle_1 < 0$ and $\triangle_2 < 0$ the productivity coefficients are of ascending order.

*Case III* : $P_n$ is not affected by a change in w or r. This is possible when $\phi$ (i) = 0 for all i which implies $\triangle_1 = 0$, $\triangle_2 = 0$ *i.e.* the productivity coefficients are equal in the capital goods sector. In this case the technology matrix is said to be Neutral Wicksell type.

The productivity coefficients of a technique with 3 departments in the capital goods sector, may be neither ascending, descending nor constant order, as in the Matrix E below.

TECHNOLOGY MATRIX E

| Man | C | $e_1$ | $e_2$ | $e_3$ | | C | $e_1$ | $e_2$ | $e_3$ |
|---|---|---|---|---|---|---|---|---|---|
| 1 | 1 | 1 | 0 | 0 | ⟶ | 10 | 1 | 0 | 0 |
| 1 | 1 | 0 | 1 | 0 | ⟶ | 0 | 4 | 1 | 0 |
| 1 | 1 | 0 | 0 | 1 | ⟶ | 0 | 0 | 2 | 1 |
| 1 | 1 | 0 | 0 | 1 | ⟶ | 0 | 0 | 0 | 3 + 1 |

For the technique E, $\phi$ (i) = i $b_2 \triangle_1 + i^2 \triangle_2$

is $i \times 2 \times 1 + i^2 (-1)$

*i.e.* $\phi$ (i) $= 2i - i^2$

$\phi$ (i) $= 2 - i$

or $\phi$ (i) = 0 at i = 2

Also, $\phi$ (i) for i > 2 is negative and $\phi$ (i) for i < 2 is positive. Thus, $\phi$ (i) < 0 for some values of i and $\phi$ (i) > 0 for higher value of i.

The technology E would, therefore, show a Positive Wicksell Response for some values of i and change its Wicksell response to Negative Wicksell Effect at still higher rates of interest.

Further, as $\phi$ (i) = 2 − i, is linear in i, the number of turning points of $P_3$ can only be one. In other words the price of the highest order equipment can be lower than higher (or *vice versa*) with respect to C, when higher and higher interest rates are considered.

If the technique has 4 capital goods, the model becomes capable of showing further complications in changes in the structure of relative price of the highest order good in relation to the consumption good. For, in this case,

$$\phi\ (i) = i\, b_2\, b_3 \triangle_1 + i^2\, b_3 \triangle_2 + i^3 \triangle_3$$

where, $\triangle_1 = (b_1 - b_4),\ \triangle_2 = (b_2 - b_4),\ \triangle_3 = (b_3 - b_4)$

Since, $\phi\ (i) = b_2\, b_3 \triangle_1 + 2\, i\, b_3 \triangle_2 + 3\, i^2 \triangle_3$

in this case, $\phi$ (i) = 0 will have two roots. Therefore, four capital goods model can have 2 turning points of $P_4$ (price of the highest order good). Hence, as higher and higher interest rates are considered the price of ($P_4$) can emerge higher, lower and higher once again, in terms of the consumption good C, although the technique is constant.

The fundamental equation also connects wr (compounded wage) with rate of profit (or rate of growth) through output per man equipment team or productivities.[12] Given any technique of production its w-r curve can be traced with the help of this equation.

However, a technique w-r curve is conditioned by constant revaluation of goods, including fixed capital equipment in response to changes in wage rates/rates of profit. The revaluation of goods or change in structure of relative prices occur due to difference in organic composition of capital between processes in general. In Sraffa-Neumann Model, since the wage rate is kept uniform between processes and raw materials are assumed away the part played by technical productivities in influencing the change in relative prices can be studied.

It has already been established[13] that for a self-reproducing durable capital model, if the diagonal elements representing productivities is either ascending or descending order or are constant, the prices of all equipments are higher, lower or remain constant with respect to the price of corn $P_0$, in response to a higher wage rate. In these cases the Wicksell response of any one equipment can represent the Wickseil response of all others.

However, when the diagonal elements are not pure ascending, descending or constant, the technique is a combination of different Wicksell structures. In this case it has been analysed that prices of different pieces of equipment do not, in general, move in the same direction. In such cases each capital good has its own Wicksell response with respect to $P_0$. This has been termed as Robinson Effect.[14]

For a technological matrix which is combination of Wicksell structure, therefore, the Wicksell response of the highest order good no longer is representative of the Wicksell response of all orders of equipment. Since, for a given change in the wage rate, $P_n$ the price of the highest order capital good may be higher, while $P_{n-2}$ may be lower and $P_{n-3}$ may be higher.

Further, the technique as a whole would exhibit a Wicksell Effect reflected by the w-r curve, which is the resultant of the Wicksell responses of different equipments used in the different processes forming a technique of production. Thus, in general the path traced out (w-r curve) by any technique is conditioned by Wicksell responses of different pieces of equipment used within a technique.

*One Capital Good Model* : Since the one capital good model at uniform wage can only exhibit Neutral Wicksell Effect, its w-r curve* would be in straight line as in figure 16.

*NOTE : As in Sraffa-Neumann Model, wage is paid in advance of production, w-r is measured on the y-axis. In Sraffa system when wage is paid post factum, w is measured on y-axis.

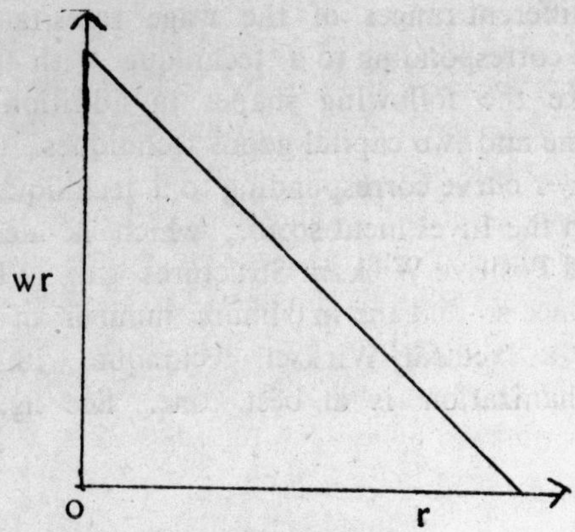


Fig. (16)

*Two Capital Goods Model* : As it was seen that a two capital good model can either be Positive Wicksell or Negative Wicksell structure in addition to Neutral Wicksell structure, the w-r curve in this case can be either convex or concave to the origin as in figure (17) and figure (18) depending upon the ordering of the productivities.

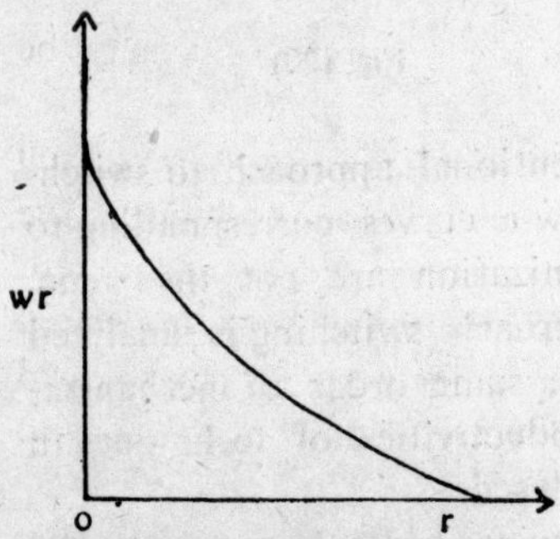


Fig. (17)

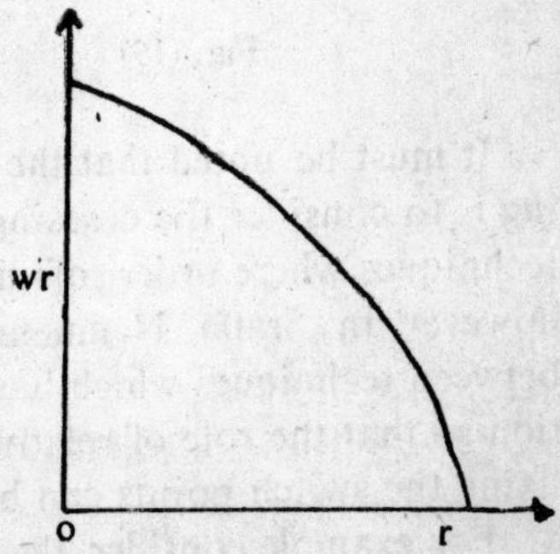


Fig. (18)

*Three Capital Goods Model*: When the number of departments in the capital goods sector is three, the w-r curve can take complex shapes apart from being concave, convex to the origin or being a straight line. This is due to the fact that in this case, the same technique can exhibit different Wicksell responses at different ranges of the wage rates/rates of profit. The w-r curve corresponding to a technique with three capital goods can take the following shapes in addition to shapes discussed in one and two capital goods techniques.

Thus, the w-r curve corresponding to a technique with three departments in the Investment sector, which is a combination of Reverse and Positive Wicksell Structures can at best change its convexity once so that the maximum number of switches it can have with a Neutral Wicksell technique with the same order of mechanization is at best one. See fig. (19) and fig. (20).

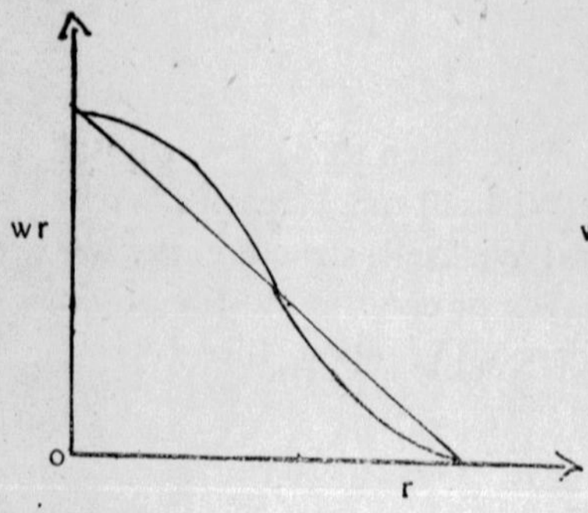


Fig. (19)

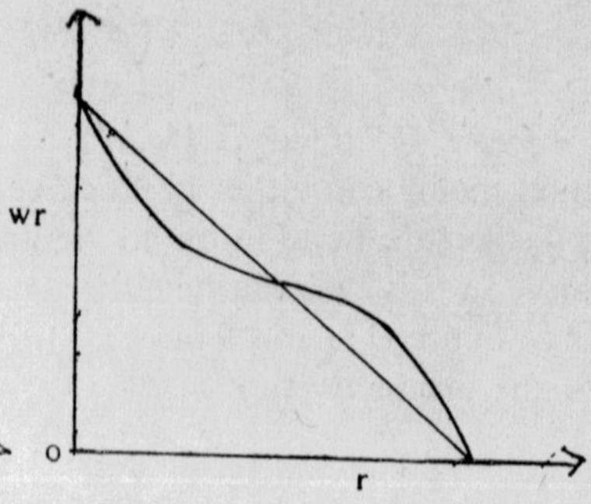


Fig. (20)

It must be noted that the conventional approach to switching is to consider the crossing of w-r curves corresponding to techniques where order of mechanization are not the same, however, in Sraffa Neumann approach switching is analysed between techniques which have the same order of mechanization so that the role of relative productivities of techniques in fixing the switch points can be analysed.

For example consider the following technology where the productivities are $b_1$, $b_2$, $b_3$ and $\triangle_1 = (b_1 - b_3)$, $\triangle_2 = (b_2 - b_3)$. The fundamental equation connecting w-r and rate of interest through productivities when reduced to three capital goods is,

$$wr = \frac{b_0\, b_1\, b_2}{b_1\, b_2\, b_3 - [i \triangle_1 b_2 + i^2 \triangle_2]}$$

If $\phi$ (i) $=$ i $\triangle_1$ $b_2$ $+$ $i^2$ $\triangle_2$, it is obvious that the w-r curve is a straight line when $\phi$ (i) $=$ 0 for all i. It is also clear that in case $\phi$ (i) $\neq$ 0 for all i, since it cuts the Neutral Wicksell Technique with the same order of mechanization when it switches with it, at the switch point $\phi$ (i) $=$ 0.

Thus, at the switch point,

$$\phi\ (i) = i\ b_2\ \triangle_1 + i^2\ \triangle_2 = 0$$

$$\text{or } i\ (b_2\ \triangle_1 + i\ \triangle_2) = 0$$

$$\textit{i.e. } i = 0 \text{ or } i = -\frac{b_2\ \triangle_1}{\triangle_2}$$

which proves that at best i can take one positive value other than zero. Hence, the three capital goods technique can at best switch once with Neutral Wicksell Technology with the same order of mechanization.

*Four Capital Goods Model* : If double switching is to occur between two techniques with the same order of mechanization, the number of capital goods must necessarily be four. Consider a technique with one C-good and four capital goods. With productivities as $b_o$, $b_1$, $b_2$, $b_3$ and $b_4$, where,

$$\triangle_1 = b_1 - b_4,\ \triangle_2 = b_2 - b_4,\ \triangle_3 = b_3 - b_4.$$

Since at a switch point $\phi$ (i) $=$ 0 and for four capital goods model,

$$\phi\ (i) = i\ b_2\ b_3\ \triangle_1 + i^2\ b_3\ \triangle_2 + i^3\ \triangle_3,\ \textit{i.e.},$$

$$i\ (b_2\ b_3\ \triangle_1 + i\ b_3\ \triangle_2 + i^2\ \triangle_3) = 0$$

$$\textit{i.e., } \text{either } i = 0 \text{ or } \quad D = \begin{bmatrix} \triangle_1 & -\triangle_2 & \triangle_3 \\ i & b_2 & 0 \\ 0 & i & b_3 \end{bmatrix} = 0$$

The necessary condition for double switching, is therefore, that the equation $D=0$ must have two real and positive roots.

A technique which is a combination of Wicksell structure, must necessarily have $\phi$ (i) $= 0$ at the point where it switches with a Neutral Wicksell Technology with the same order of mechanization, which implies that at the switch point the prices of the first order and $n^{th}$ order equipments in the technique are equal at some rate of interest, (at which the switch is taking place). Since a Technology which is a combination of different Wicksell structures will not have $\phi$ (i) $= 0$ for all i, and each equipment will have its own Wicksell response, therefore if, $\phi$ (i) $= 0$ at $i = \bar{i}$, the prices of equipments have to be equal at $i = \bar{i}$, termed as crossing of prices of Sraffa Effect.[15] Crossing of prices necessarily calls for a change in the Wicksell response of the highest order good $P_4$, at some interest rate $i < \bar{i}$. Thus, for every switch point say $s_1 = i$, there is a corresponding rate of interest $i < \bar{i}$ where a change in the Wicksell Response of the highest order good takes place. Therefore, Robinson Effect precedes Sraffa Effect.

If a technological structure is to be analysed further in order to get insight into the relationship between relative productivities ($\triangle$s) and the position of switch points, the logical starting point would be to study the relationship between $\triangle$s and the number of turning points that $P_4$ has in response to changes in distribution. In other words the relationship between $\triangle$s and Robinson Effect.

In the four sector case the sufficient condition for double switching is that $\phi$ (i) $= 0$, has two roots between 0 and $b_4$. This calls for two turning points between 0 and $b_4$ of the price of the highest order equipment $P_4$.

Therefore, the conditions for a technique with 4-sectors in the Investment department to have two turning points of the price of the highest order equipment, $P_4$ was analysed. It was found that the technique must necessarily be either of type F or type G as follows :

| F | G |
|---|---|
| $b_0 = b_0$ | $b_0 = b_0$ |
| $b_1 < b_4$ | $b_1 > b_4$ |
| $b_2 > b_4$ | $b_2 < b_4$ |
| $b_3 < b_4$ | $b_3 > b_4$ |
| $b_4 = b_4$ | $b_4 = b_4$ |

For example the necessary condition demands* that the technique be either like the matrix F or matrix G.

TECHNOLOGY MATRIX F

| Men | C | $e_1$ | $e_2$ | $e_3$ | $e_4$ | | C | $e_1$ | $e_2$ | $e_3$ | $e_4$ |
|---|---|---|---|---|---|---|---|---|---|---|---|
| 1 | 1 | 1 | 0 | 0 | 0 | $\longrightarrow$ | 25 | 1 | 0 | 0 | 0 |
| 1 | 1 | 0 | 1 | 0 | 0 | $\longrightarrow$ | 0 | $b_1<6$ | 1 | 0 | 0 |
| 1 | 1 | 0 | 0 | 1 | 0 | $\longrightarrow$ | 0 | 0 | $b_2>6$ | 1 | 0 |
| 1 | 1 | 0 | 0 | 0 | 1 | $\longrightarrow$ | 0 | 0 | 0 | $b_3<6$ | 1 |
| 1 | 1 | 0 | 0 | 0 | 1 | $\longrightarrow$ | 0 | 0 | 0 | 0 | 5+1 |

Where $b_1$ and $b_3$ will have to take values subject to an upper limit 6 and $b_2$ has 6 as the lower limit.

TECHNOLOGY MATRIX G

| Men | C | $e_1$ | $e_2$ | $e_3$ | $e_4$ | | C | $e_1$ | $e_2$ | $e_3$ | $e_4$ |
|---|---|---|---|---|---|---|---|---|---|---|---|
| 1 | 1 | 1 | 0 | 0 | 0 | $\longrightarrow$ | 25 | 1 | 0 | 0 | 0 |
| 1 | 1 | 0 | 1 | 0 | 0 | $\longrightarrow$ | 0 | $b_1>6$ | 1 | 0 | 0 |
| 1 | 1 | 0 | 0 | 1 | 0 | $\longrightarrow$ | 0 | 0 | $b_2<6$ | 1 | 0 |
| 1 | 1 | 0 | 0 | 0 | 1 | $\longrightarrow$ | 0 | 0 | 0 | $b_3>6$ | 1 |
| 1 | 1 | 0 | 0 | 0 | 1 | $\longrightarrow$ | 0 | 0 | 0 | 0 | 5+1 |

*See Appendix for rigorous derivation of the necessary and sufficient conditions.

In this case $b_1$ and $b_3$ have a lower limit as 6 and $b_2$ has 6 as the upper limit.

It was seen that when a non-Neutral Wicksell Technology crosses the path of a Neutral Wicksell Technology of the same order of mechanization, switches occur. For example in the diagram below (21), $\alpha$ technique crosses $\beta$ technique twice, at a and b.

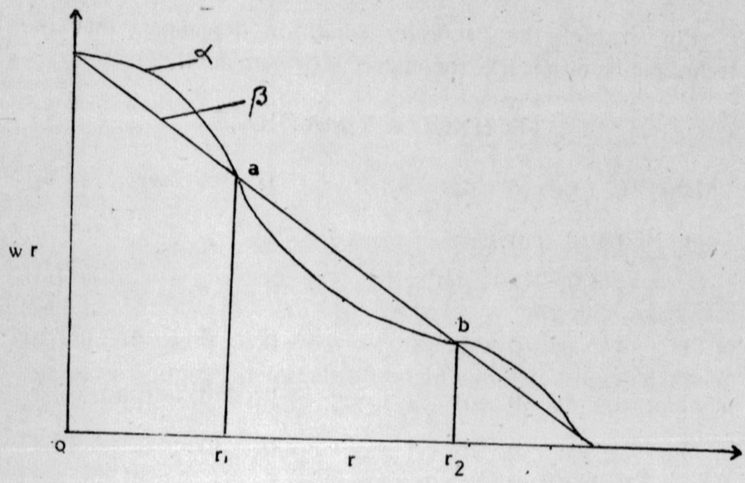


Fig. (21)

At a and b where switches occur, it is essential that prices cross, for the technique $\alpha$, as it is a non-Neutral Wicksell Technology. In other words Sraffa Effect must take place at interest rates $s_1$ and $s_2$. But for prices to cross at $s_1$ and $s_2$, at some $r < s_1$, $P_4$ must change its Wicksell effect from reverse to positive as in Fig. (22), and if Prices cross at $s_2$, $P_4$ must change its Wicksell structure from positive to reverse once again for $r < s_2$ [see Fig. (22)]. Therefore, for prices to cross the Wicksell response of $P_4$ must necessarily change, this change in Wicksell response has been termed as Robinson Effect. As the Robinson Effect forms the basis for Switches to occur, the role played by relative productivities, $\Delta_1=(b_1-b_4)$, $\Delta_2=(b_2-b_4)$. $\Delta_3=(b_3-b_4)$ in shifting the turning points of Wicksell response of $P_4$ was analysed.

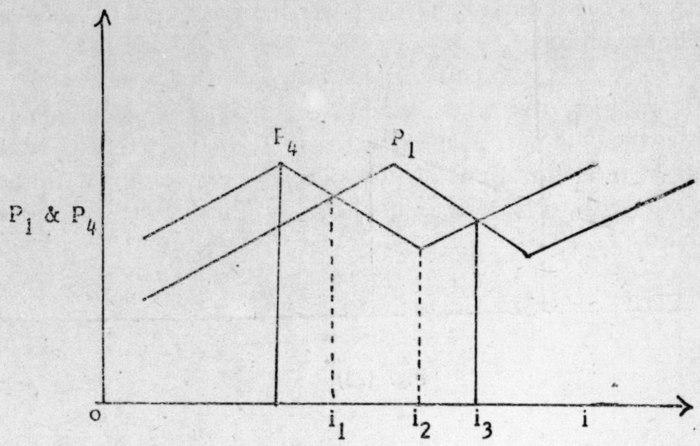


Fig. (22)

Techniques that do not satisfy the necessary condition for double switching were taken up to start with, for the analysis of the relationship between $\triangle$s and the turning points of Wicksell response of the highest order good $P_4$. For example, if the technology (7, 10, 1, 6) is considered, $\phi$ (i) = 0 has two roots, $i_1$ = 1.13 and $i_2$ = $-$0.59, see Table (1). $P_4$ changes its Wicksell structure at two different rates of interest but only one of them where i is positive has economic significance namely, at $i_1$ = 1.13, when shown on a diagram, the turning points will be as in Fig. (23) on page 110.

The corresponding switch points lie at i = —1.8 and i = 1.86. The positive switch point corresponding to i = 1.13 which is 1.08 is shown in Fig. (24) and Table (2).

To study the effect of a change in $b_3$ on switch points, the technology (7, 10, 3, 6) was considered (higher $b_3$, all other, productivities remaining constant). For this technology, solving $\phi'$ (i) = 0, the turning points of $P_4$ are found to be at i = 3.59 and i = —0.93 see Table (1). The switch point for the technology corresponding to the positive turning point i = 3.59 lies at i = 5.77 as in Fig. (26) and Table (2).

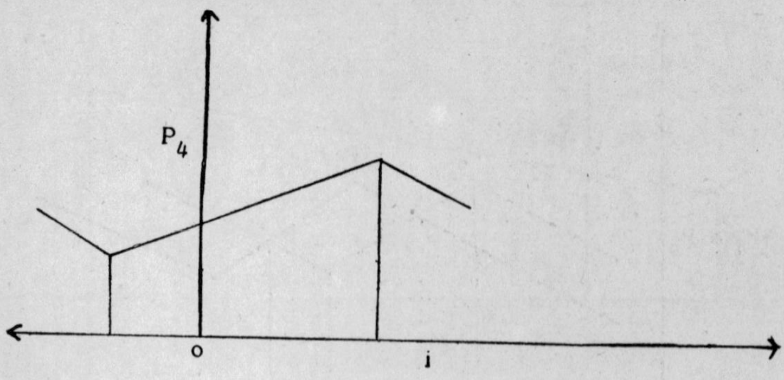


Fig. (23)

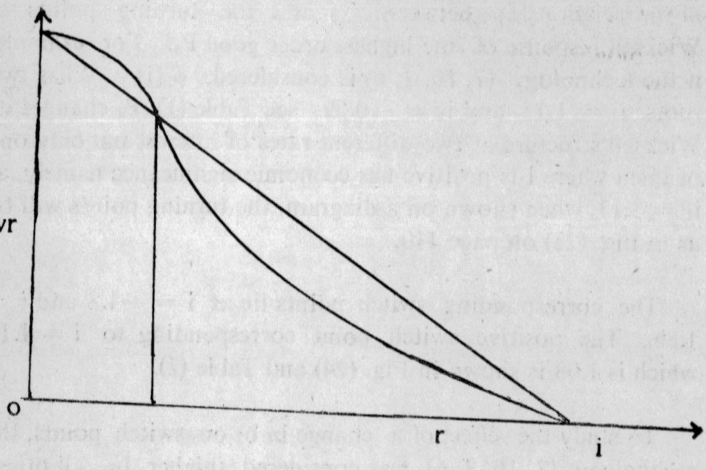


Fig. (24)

If $b_3$ is taken still higher ($b_3 = 4$) the positive turning point of $P_4$ lies at 6.38 and the corresponding switch point lies at i = 10.0, as in Fig. (27). This case is not of any economic significance as the switch at i = 10, is for negative values of w-r.

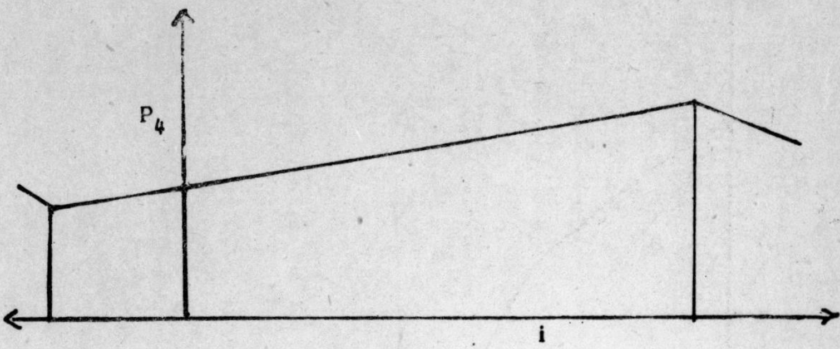


Fig. (25)

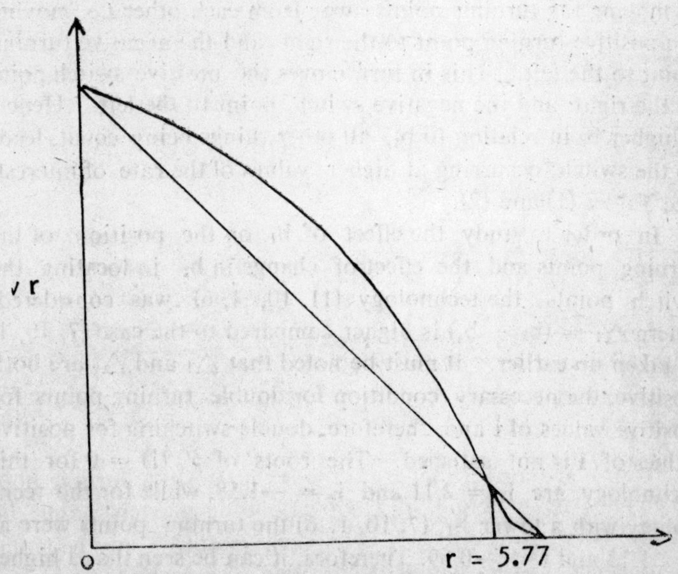


Fig. (26)

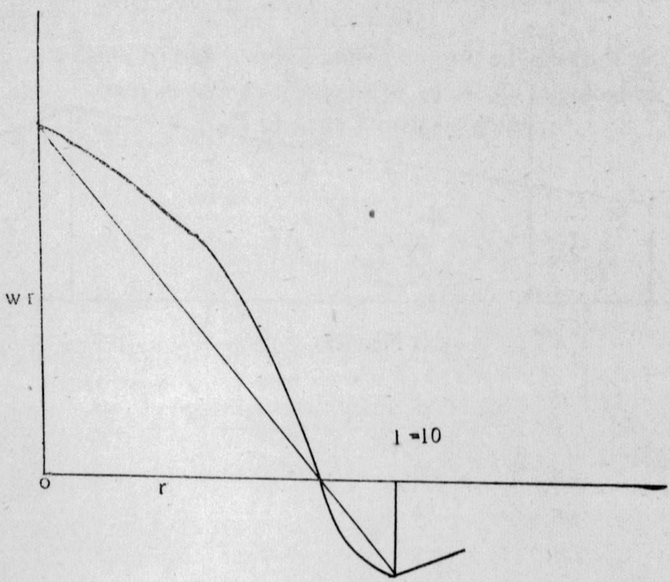


Fig. (27)

Thus, higher relative values of $b_2$, $(b_3 - b_4)$ has the effect of moving the turning points away from each other *i.e.* moving the positive turning point to the right and the negative turning point to the left. This in turn moves the positive switch point to the right and the negative switch point to the left. Hence, a higher $b_3$ in relation to $b_4$, all other things being equal, leads to the switch occurring at higher values of the rate of interest. See Tables (1) and (2).

In order to study the effect of $b_1$ on the position of the turning points and the effect of change in $b_1$ in locating the switch points, the technology (11, 10, 1, 6) was considered, where $\triangle_1 = (b_1 - b_4)$ is higher compared to the case (7, 10, 1, 6) taken up earlier. It must be noted that $\triangle_1$ and $\triangle_2$ are both positive, the necessary condition for double turning points for positive values of i and, therefore, double switching for positive values of i is not satisfied. The roots of $\phi'$ (i) = 0 for this technology are $i_1 = 2.11$ and $i_2 = -1.58$, while for the technology with a lower $b_1$, (7, 10, 1, 6) the turning points were at i = 1.13 and i = —0.59. Therefore, it can be seen that a higher $b_1$ has the same effect as a higher $b_3$ namely, the real and

TABLE 1

Table showing the turning points (roots $i_1$ and $i_2$) for the technologies (7, 10, $b_3$, 6) when $\triangle_1 = 1$ as $b_3$ takes integer values from 1 to 20.

| $b_3$ | $\triangle_3$ | Roots $i_1$ | $i_2$ |
|---|---|---|---|
| \| 1 | –5 | 1.13 \| | –0.59 |
| \| 2 | –4 | 2.12 \| | –0.79 |
| \| 3 | –3 | 3.59 \| | –0.93 |
| 4 | –2 | 6.38 | –1.05 |
| 5 | –1 | 14.50 | –1.15 |
| 6 | 0 | — | –1.5 |
| 7 | 1 | –17.32 | –1.35 |
| 8 | 2 | –9.22 | –1.44 |
| 9 | 3 | –6.45 | –1.55 |
| 10 | 4 | –5.00 | –1.67 |
| 11 | 5 | –4.06 | –1.81 |
| 12 | 6 | –3.33 | –2.00 |
| 13 | 7 | Imaginary | |
| 14 | 8 | do | |
| 15 | 9 | do | |
| 16 | 10 | do | |
| 17 | 11 | do | |
| 18 | 12 | do | |
| 19 | 13 | do | |
| 20 | 14 | do | |

|_____| —Effective Range.

TABLE 2

Table showing the switch points (roots $s_1$ and $s_2$ of $\phi$ (i) = 0) for the technologies (7, 10, $b_3$, 6) when $\triangle_1$ = 1, as $b_3$ takes integer values from 1 to 20.

| $b_3$ | 3 | Roots $s_1$ | $s_2$ |
|---|---|---|---|
| 1 | —5 | 1.860 | —1.880 |
| 2 | —4 | 3.500 | —1.500 |
| 3 | —3 | 5.770 | —1.780 |
| 4 | —2 | 10.000 | —2.000 |
| 5 | —1 | 16.125 | —3.875 |
| 6 | 0 | — | — |
| 7 | 1 | —11.875 | —16.125 |
| 8 | 2 | —3.100 | —12.900 |
| 9 | 3 | —3.550 | —8.450 |
| 10 | 4 | —2.500 | —4.230 |
| 11 | 5 | Not Real | |
| 12 | 6 | do | |
| 13 | 7 | do | |
| 14 | 8 | do | |
| 15 | 9 | do | |
| 16 | 10 | do | |
| 17 | 11 | do | |
| 18 | 12 | do | |
| 19 | 13 | do | |
| 20 | 14 | do | |

|___| — Effective Range.

positive turning points shift to the right and the negative turning point shifts to the left, see Table (3). The corresponding switch points are $i = 3.5880$ and $i = -2.7880$ when $b_1$ is taken higher, see Table 4. Comparing these values of i at which switch points lie with the values of i for the technology (7, 10, 1, 6), $i = 1.86$ and $i = -1.8$ the effect of a higher $b_1$ on the location of switch points. becomes clear, namely, a higher $b_1$ shifts the switch points away from each other.

When $b_1 = 16$ is considered, *i.e.* the technology (16, 10, 1, 6), where the productivity of $b_1$ is much higher compared to (7, 10, 1, 6), the turning points lie at $i = 2.86$ and $i = -2.33$. Comparing these with the turning points of (11, 10, 1, 6) which are at $i = 2.11$ and $i = -1.58$ it can be seen that a higher $\triangle_1 = (b_1 - b_4)$ has the effect of shifting the roots of $\phi'(i) = 0$ away from each other and therefore, the switch points also lie at greater values of i, for $i = 4.8900$ and $i = -4.0900$ [see Tables (5) and (6)].

**Double-Robinson Effect Technologies**

In order to analyse the impact of changed $\triangle$s, or relative productivities on the location of switch points, the technology (7, 1, 14, 6) which satisfies the necessary condition for two turning points of $P_4$ for positive values of i istaken as the standard. As expected, $\phi'(i) = 0$ for this technology has two positive roots, $i = 0.102$ and $i = 5.732$, the corresponding switch points lie at $i = 0.21$, $i = 8.54$. It can be seen in Figs. (27) and (28) that out of the two positive switch points, one is for negative values of wr, $i = 8.54$. Thus, the necessary condition for double switch points, may not be sufficient to give rise to two switch points which have economic significance.

If the technology (7, 1, 20, 6) is considered the roots of $\phi'(i) = 0$ are $i = 0.102$, $i = 4.659$ the corresponding switch-points are $i = 0.21$, $i = 6.93$ [ see Tables (7) and (8) ]. As $b_3$ is higher, the switch points move towards each other, but $b_3 = 20$ is not high enough to meet the sufficient condition of two roots of i between zero and six. If $b_3$ is as high as 33, *i.e.* (7, 1, 33, 6) the roots of the equation $\phi(i) = 0$ are $i = 0.21$ and $i = 5.86$, the switch points are closer, and lie between $0 < i < 6$ [see Table (8)].

TABLE 3

Table showing the turning points (roots $i_1$ and $i_2$) for the technologies (11, 10, $b_3$, 6) as $b_3$ takes integer values from 1 to 20.

| $b_3$ | $\Delta_3$ | Roots $i_1$ | $i_2$ |
|---|---|---|---|
| 1 | —5 | 2.11 | —1.58 |
| 2 | —4 | 3.63 | —2.30 |
| 3 | —3 | 5.63 | —2.26 |
| 4 | —2 | 9.03 | —3.69 |
| 5 | —1 | 18,00 | —4.64 |
| 6 | 0 | — | —6.25 |
| 7 | 1 | Imaginary | |
| 8 | 2 | do | |
| 9 | 3 | do | |
| 10 | 4 | do | |
| 11 | 5 | do | |
| 12 | 6 | do | |
| 13 | 7 | do | |
| 14 | 8 | do | |
| 15 | 9 | do | |
| 16 | 10 | do | |
| 17 | 11 | do | |
| 18 | 12 | do | |
| 19 | 13 | do | |
| 20 | 14 | do | |

— Effective Range.

Comparing Tables (1) and (2) to find the effect of change in $\Delta_1$ (*i.e.* $\Delta_1$ higher) it can be seen that,

1. $\Delta_1$ increasing makes the real and positive turning point shift *rightward.* (The turning point lies at a greater value of i).
2. $b_3$ can take values upto 3 [see Table (3)] *i.e.* the possible technologies are, (11, 10, 1, 6), (11, 10, 2, 6) and (11, 10, 3, 6).

TABLE 4

Table showing the switch points (roots $s_1$ and $s_2$ of $\phi$ (i) = 0), for the technologies (11, 10, $b_3$, 6) when $\triangle_1$ = 5, as $b_3$ takes integer values from 1 to 20.

| $b_3$ | $\triangle_3$ | Roots $s_1$ | $s_2$ |
|---|---|---|---|
| 1 | —5 | 3.5880 | —2.7880 |
| 2 | —4 | 6.1000 | —4.1000 |
| 3 | —3 | 9.3500 | —5.3500 |
| 4 | —2 | 14.8000 | —6.8000 |
| 5 | —1 | 28.7250 | —8.7250 |
| 6 | 0 | — | — |
| 7 | 1 | Not real | |
| 8 | 2 | do | |
| 9 | 3 | do | |
| 10 | 4 | do | |
| 11 | 5 | do | |
| 12 | 6 | do | |
| 13 | 7 | do | |
| 14 | 8 | do | |
| 15 | 9 | do | |
| 16 | 10 | do | |
| 17 | 11 | do | |
| 18 | 12 | do | |
| 19 | 13 | do | |
| 20 | 14 | do | |

└─┘ — Effective Range.

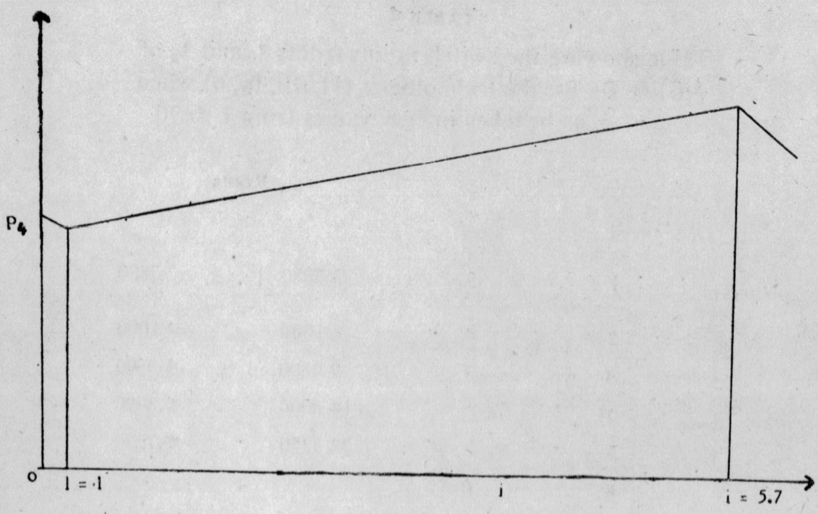


Fig. (28)

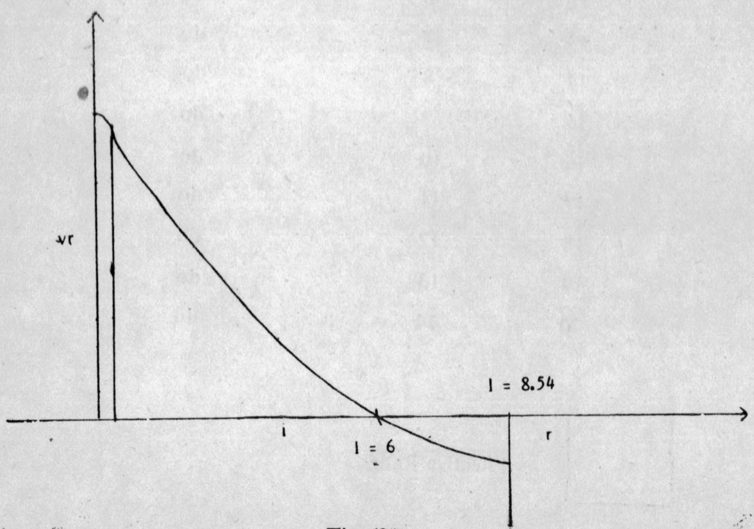


Fig. (29)

TABLE 5

Table showing the turning points (roots $i_1$ and $i_2$) for the technologies (16, 10, $b_3$, 6) as $b_3$ takes integer values from 1 to 20.

| $b_3$ | $\Delta_3$ | Roots $i_1$ | Roots $i_2$ |
|---|---|---|---|
| 1 | —5 | 2.86 | —2.33 |
| 2 | —4 | 4.80 | —3.47 |
| 3 | —3 | 7.27 | —4.59 |
| 4 | —2 | 11.26 | —5.92 |
| 5 | —1 | 21.20 | —7.86 |
| 6 | 0 | — | —12.50 |
| 7 | 1 | Imaginary | |
| 8 | 2 | do | |
| 9 | 3 | do | |
| 10 | 4 | do | |
| 11 | 5 | do | |
| 12 | 6 | do | |
| 13 | 7 | do | |
| 14 | 8 | do | |
| 15 | 9 | do | |
| 16 | 10 | do | |
| 17 | 11 | do | |
| 18 | 12 | do | |
| 19 | 13 | do | |
| 20 | 14 | do | |

|__| — Effective Range.

TABLE 6

Table showing the switch points (roots $s_1$ and $s_2$) of (i) = 0, for the technologies (16, 10, $b_3$, 6) when $\triangle_1 = 5$ as $b_3$ takes integer values from 1 to 20.

| $b_3$ | $\triangle_3$ | Roots $s_1$ | $s_2$ |
|---|---|---|---|
| 1 | —5 | 4.8900 | —4.0900 |
| 2 | —4 | 8.1500 | —6.1500 |
| 3 | —3 | 12.1666 | —8.1666 |
| 4 | —2 | 18.7000 | —10.7000 |
| 5 | —1 | 34.9000 | —14.9000 |
| 6 | 0 | — | — |
| 7 | 1 | Not Real | |
| 8 | 2 | do | |
| 9 | 3 | do | |
| 10 | 4 | do | |
| 11 | 5 | do | |
| 12 | 6 | do | |
| 13 | 7 | do | |
| 14 | 8 | do | |
| 15 | 9 | do | |
| 16 | 10 | do | |
| 17 | 11 | do | |
| 18 | 12 | do | |
| 19 | 13 | do | |
| 20 | 14 | do | |

— Effective Range.

**Table 7**

Table showing the turning points (roots $i_1$ and $i_2$ of $\phi'(i) = 0$) for the technologies (7, 1, $b_3$, 6) when $\triangle_1 = 1$, $\triangle_2 = -5$, as $b_3$ takes integer values from 1 to 20.

| $b_3$ | $\triangle_3$ | Roots $i_1$ | Roots $i_2$ |
|---|---|---|---|
| 1 | —5 | 0.08830368 | —0.7549703 |
| 2 | —4 | 0.09462726 | —1.7612940 |
| 3 | —3 | 0.09716748 | —3.4305010 |
| 4 | —2 | 0.09854268 | —6.7652110 |
| 5 | —1 | 0.09945280 | —16.7660700 |
| 6 | 0 | ... | 0.1000000 |
| 7 | 1 | 0.10043330 | 23.2329000 |
| 8 | 2 | 0.10076230 | 13.2325700 |
| 9 | 3 | 0.10101980 | 9.8989790 |
| 10 | 4 | 0.10122960 | 8.2321040 |
| 11 | 5 | 0.10140220 | 7.2319330 |
| 12 | 6 | 0.10154670 | 6.5651190 |
| 13 | 7 | 0.10166930 | 6.0888060 |
| 14 | 8 | 0.10177610 | 5.7315570 |
| 15 | 9 | 0.10186810 | 5.4536870 |
| 16 | 10 | 0.10194870 | 5.2313840 |
| 17 | 11 | 0.10202070 | 5.0494940 |
| 18 | 12 | 0.10208410 | 4.8979150 |
| 19 | 13 | 0.10214180 | 4.7696530 |
| 20 | 14 | 0.10219330 | 4.6597110 |

(Rows 14–20 are enclosed by vertical bars marking the effective range.)

—— Effective Range

TABLE 8

Table showing the switch points, (roots $s_1$ and $s_2$ of $\phi$ (i) = 0) for the technologies (7, 1, $b_3$, 6) as $b_3$ takes integer values from 1 to 33.

| $b_3$ | 3 | Roots $s_1$ | Roots $s_2$ |
|---|---|---|---|
| 1 | —5 | 0.62 | —1.62 |
| 2 | —4 | 0.18 | —2.68 |
| 3 | —3 | 0.18 | —5.18 |
| 4 | —2 | 0.20 | —10.92 |
| 5 | —1 | 0.20 | —25.20 |
| 6 | 0 | . . . | . . . |
| 7 | 1 | 0.20 | 34.80 |
| 8 | 2 | 0.21 | 19.79 |
| 9 | 3 | 0.21 | 14.79 |
| 10 | 4 | 0.21 | 12.29 |
| 11 | 5 | 0.21 | 10.79 |
| 12 | 6 | 0.21 | 9.79 |
| 13 | 7 | 0.21 | 9.08 |
| 14 | 8 | 0.21 | 8.54 |
| 15 | 9 | 0.21 | 8.13 |
| 16 | 10 | 0.21 | 7.79 |
| 17 | 11 | 0.21 | 7.52 |
| 18 | 12 | 0.21 | 7.29 |
| 19 | 13 | 0.21 | 7.10 |
| 20 | 14 | 0.21 | 6.93 |
| .. | .. | .. | .. |
| .. | .. | .. | .. |
| 30 | 24 | 0.21 | 6.04 |
| \| 31 | 25 | 0.21 | 5.99 \| |
| \| 32 | 26 | 0.21 | 5.90 \| |
| \| 33 | 27 | 0.21 | 5.86 \| |

⊓ ——Effective Range

Next the technology (11, 1, 20, 6) is taken up for analysis, where $\triangle_1$ is higher compared to (7, 1, 20, 6). The turning points or the roots of $\phi'$ (i) = 0 for this technology are i = 0.57 and i = 4.9 [see Table (9) ], while for the technology (7, 1, 20, 6) the roots are i = 0.102 and i = 4.659.

Hence, a higher $\triangle_1$ shifts the turning points towards each other, $i_1$ rightward and $i_2$ leftward, and therefore, the corresponding switch points $s_1$ and $s_2$ towards each other, the roots of $\phi$ (i) = 0 for this technology being i = 0.214, i = 5.929 as against the switch points for (7, 1, 20, 6) which are at i = 0.21, i = 6.93.

Further, as $b_1$ is higher ($\triangle_1 \uparrow$)the values of $b_3$ for which double switching occurs are lower. For example when $b_1$ = 7, $b_3$ had to be 33 for both switches to be positive and lie between 0< i <6, when $b_1$ = 11, for the technology (11, 1, 20, 6) the switch points lie i = 0.21, i = 0.5929 [see Table (10) ].

If higher values of $b_1$ are considered, $b_3$ can take lower values to get two turning points of $P_4$ well within the range 0< i <6 so as to give rise to two switch points $s_1$ and $s_2$ also within the range 0< i <6. Thus, the technology (16, 1, 15, 6) gives two roots of $\phi'$ (i) = 0, $i_1$ = 1.31, $i_2$ = 4.25. The corresponding switch points are given by roots of $\phi$ (i) = 0, which are $s_1$ = 3.330 and $s_2$ = 5.000 [see Tables (11) and (12) and Figs. (29) and (30) ].

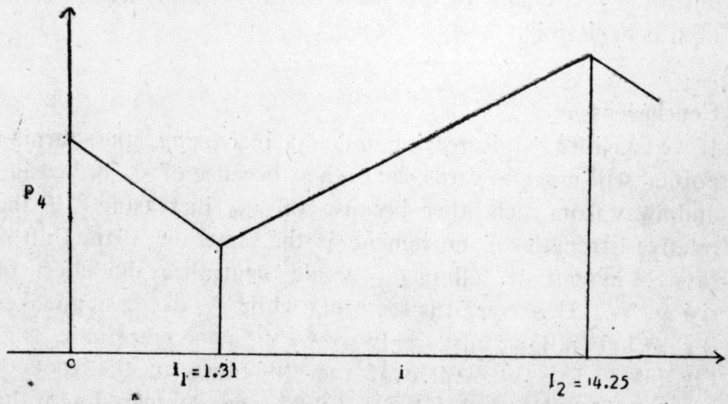


Fig. (30)

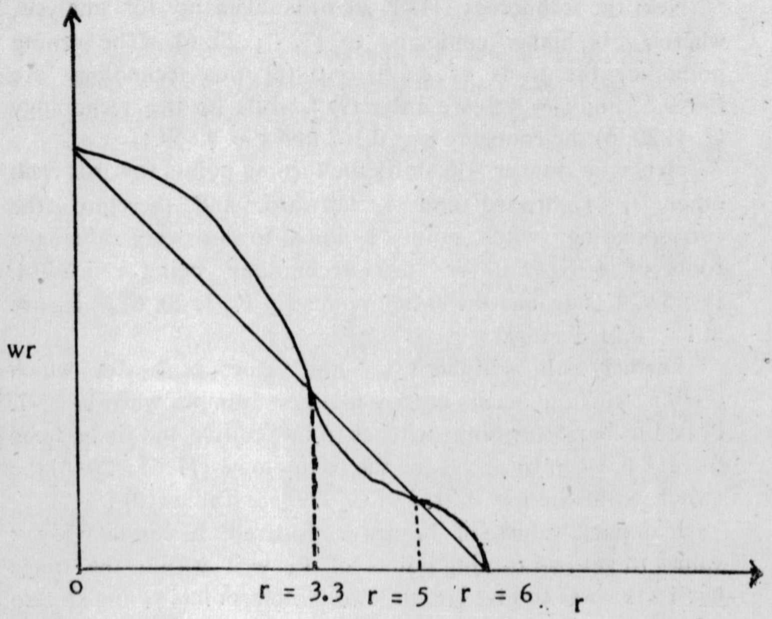


Fig. (31)

A careful study of the tables would also reveal that as $\triangle_1$ increases $s_1$ and $s_2$ converge with the magnitude of the shift being equal, while a higher $\triangle_3$ shifts $s_2$ leftward and $s_1$ rightward, but the leftward shift of $s_2$ is marked while the rightward shift of $s_1$ is negligible.

**Conclusions**

If we consider $\triangle_1$ decreasing and $\triangle_3$ increasing, the turning points will move towards each other, because of $\triangle_1$ decreasing and away from each other because of $\triangle_3$ increasing. If the relative strength of movement is the same, i.e., if the shift is same in magnitude, falling $\triangle_1$ would neutralise the effect of rising $\triangle_3$. However, it is seen that while $\triangle_1$ decreasing makes $i_1$ shift leftward, $i_2$ shifts rightward by the *same magnitude*, as in Fig. (31). This is evident if the difference in the roots of $i_1$ of Tables (1) and (3) are found and compared with the difference in the roots of $i_2$ of Tables (1) and (3).

TABLE 9

Table showing the turning points (roots $i_1$ and $i_2$ of $\phi'(i) = 0$) for the technologies (11, 1, $b_3$, 6) when $\triangle_1 = 5$ and $\triangle_2 = -5$ as $b_3$ takes integer values from 1 to 20.

| $b_3$ | $\triangle_3$ | Roots $i_1$ | Roots $i_2$ |
|---|---|---|---|
| 1 | —5 | 0.33 | —1.00 |
| 2 | —4 | 0.40 | —2.07 |
| 3 | —3 | 0.44 | —3.78 |
| 4 | —2 | 0.47 | —7.13 |
| 5 | —1 | 0.49 | −17.15 |
| 6 | 0 | 0.50 | . . . |
| 7 | 1 | 0.51 | 22.82 |
| 8 | 2 | 0.52 | 12.81 |
| 9 | 3 | 0.53 | 9.47 |
| 10 | 4 | 0.53 | 7.80 |
| 11 | 5 | 0.54 | 6.79 |
| 12 | 6 | 0.55 | 6.12 |
| 13 | 7 | 0.55 | 5.64 |
| 14 | 8 | 0.55 | 5.28 |
| 15 | 9 | 0.56 | 5.00 |
| 16 | 10 | 0.56 | 4.77 |
| 17 | 11 | 0.56 | 4.59 |
| 18 | 12 | 0.56 | 4.44 |
| 19 | 13 | 0.57 | 4.31 |
| 20 | 14 | 0.57 | 4.19 |

⌈ ⌉ ——Effective Range (rows 13–20)

$\triangle_1$ increasing, shifts the root $i_1$ *rightward* (*i.e.* one turning point shifts rightward), while $i_2$, the other turning point moves *leftward*.

TABLE 10

Table showing the switch points (roots $s_1$ and $s_2$ of $\phi$ (i) = 0) for the technologies (11, 1, $b_3$, 6) as $b_3$ takes integer values from 1 to 23.

| $b_3$ | $\triangle_3$ | Roots $s_1$ | Roots $s_2$ |
|---|---|---|---|
| 1 | —5 | 0.62 | —1.62 |
| 2 | —4 | 0.77 | —3.27 |
| 3 | —3 | 0.85 | —5.85 |
| 4 | —2 | 0.92 | —10.92 |
| 5 | —1 | 0.96 | —25.96 |
| 6 | 0 | .. | .. |
| 7 | 1 | 1.03 | 33.97 |
| 8 | 2 | 1.05 | 18.95 |
| 9 | 3 | 1.07 | 13.93 |
| 10 | 4 | 1.10 | 11.40 |
| 11 | 5 | 1.12 | 9.885 |
| 12 | 6 | 1.12 | 8.880 |
| 13 | 7 | 1.14 | 8.145 |
| 14 | 8 | 1.151 | 7.598 |
| 15 | 9 | 1.160 | 7.170 |
| 16 | 10 | 1.168 | 6.832 |
| 17 | 11 | 1.180 | 6.546 |
| 18 | 12 | 1.187 | 6.310 |
| 19 | 13 | 1.195 | 6.112 |
| 20 | 14 | 1.214 | 5.929 |
| 21 | 15 | 1.214 | 5.800 |
| 22 | 16 | 1.214 | 5.623 |
| 23 | 17 | 1.220 | 5.545 |

(Rows 20–23 enclosed in box) = Effective Range

TABLE 11

Table showing the turning points (roots of $i_1$ and $i_2$ of $\phi'(i) = 0$) for the technologies (26, 1, $b_3$, 6) as $b_3$ takes integer values from 1 to 20.

| $b_3$ | $\triangle_3$ | Roots $i_1$ | Roots $i_2$ |
|---|---|---|---|
| 1 | —5 | 0.55 | —1.22 |
| 2 | —4 | 0.70 | —2.37 |
| 3 | —3 | 0.80 | —4.13 |
| 4 | —2 | 0.88 | —7.55 |
| 5 | —1 | 0.95 | —17.61 |
| 6 | 0 | 1.00 | ... |
| 7 | 1 | 1.05 | 22.28 |
| 8 | 2 | 1.09 | 12.24 |
| 9 | 3 | 1.13 | 8.87 |
| 10 | 4 | 1.16 | 7.17 |
| 11 | 5 | 1.19 | 6.14 |
| \| 12 | 6 | 1.23 | 5.44 \| |
| \| 13 | 7 | 1.25 | 4.93 \| |
| \| 14 | 8 | 1.28 | 4.55 \| |
| \| 15 | 9 | 1.31 | 4.25 \| |
| \| 16 | 10 | 1.33 | 4.00 \| |
| \| 17 | 11 | 1.36 | 3.79 \| |
| \| 18 | 12 | 1.38 | 3.62 \| |
| \| 19 | 13 | 1.41 | 3.47 \| |
| \| 20 | 14 | 1.43 | 3.33 \| |

| | = Effective Range

TABLE 12

Table showing the switch points (roots $s_1$ and $s_2$ of $\phi$ (i) = 0) for the technologies (16, 1, $b_3$, 6) as $b_3$ takes values from 1 to 20.

| $b_3$ | $\triangle_3$ | Roots $s_1$ | $s_2$ |
|---|---|---|---|
| 1 | –5 | 1.000 | –2.000 |
| 2 | –4 | 1.310 | –3.812 |
| 3 | –3 | 1.520 | –6.520 |
| 4 | –2 | 1.720 | –11.720 |
| 5 | –1 | 1.860 | –26.860 |
| 6 | 0 | . . . | . . . |
| 7 | 1 | 2.130 | 32.870 |
| 8 | 2 | 2.240 | 17.760 |
| 9 | 3 | 2.395 | 12.620 |
| 10 | 4 | 2.500 | 10.000 |
| 11 | 5 | 2.625 | 8.370 |
| 12 | 6 | 2.750 | 7.250 |
| 13 | 7 | 2.910 | 6.370 |
| 14 | 8 | 3.095 | 5.654 |
| 15 | 9 | 3.330 | 5.000 |
| 16 | 10 | 4.000 | . . . |
| 17 | 11 | Not Real | |
| 18 | 12 | do | |
| 19 | 13 | do | |
| 20 | 14 | do | |

= Effective Range

$\triangle_1$ increasing, shifts one switch point $s_1$ *rightward*, and the second switch point $s_2$ *leftward* i.e. the switch points converge. Further, the magnitude of the shift $s_1$ and $s_2$ are equal.

$\triangle_3$ increasing shifts $i_1$ very slightly to the *right*, it shifts $i_2$ *leftward* to a *greater* extent as shown in Fig. (32) above. Thus if $\triangle_1$ alone is increased $i_1$ and $i_2$ will move towards each other, and the magnitude of the shift will also be equal. If $\triangle_3$ alone is increased the turning points will still move towards each other, but $i_2$ moves to a greater extent to the left than $i_1$ moves rightward.

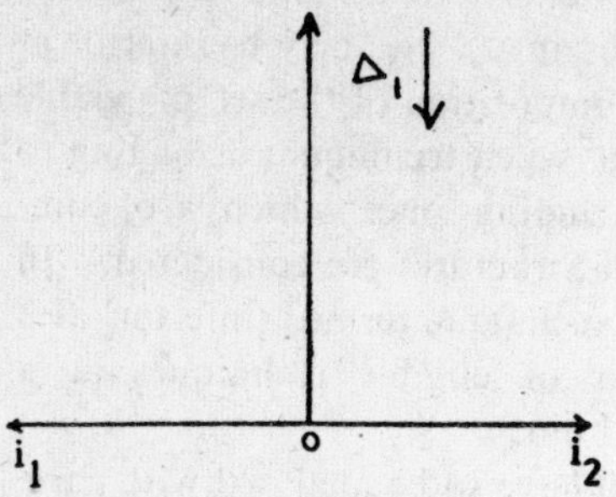


**Fig. (32)**

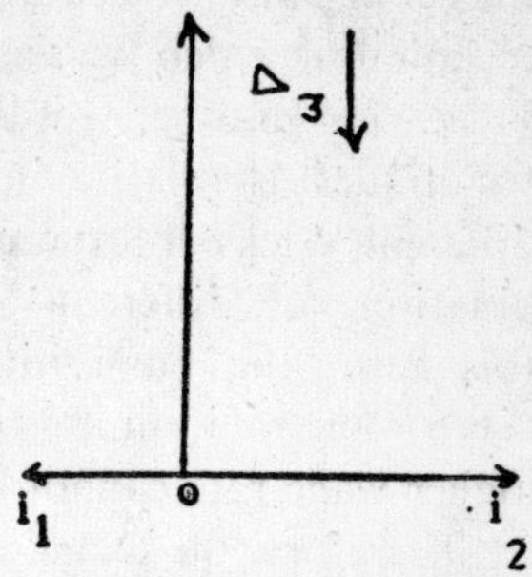


**Fig. (33)**

If $\triangle_1$ and $\triangle_3$ are both higher, then the roots of $\phi'(i) = 0$, $i_1$ and $i_2$, move towards each other, but $i_2$ moves *leftward much more than* $i_1$ *does rightward.*

As Robinson Effect in the cause of switch points, it precedes Sraffa Effect, therefore, the pattern of movement of switch points in response to changes/differences in $\triangle_5$ is similar to the movement of the turning points.

Hence, if a shift in both switches is desired, the active variable is $\triangle_1$, which brings about an equal shift in the switch points.

If a shift in $s_2$ alone is desired then the variable to be changed is $\triangle_3$ for it leaves $s_1$ almost unchanged.

Further, $\triangle_1$ high leads to double switching characteristic within 0 to $b_4$ for lower values of $b_3$. Hence, higher is the value of $\triangle_1$ and lower is $\triangle_3$ in any technique, greater are the possibilities of its double switching within the relevant wage range.

Thus, it is established that if technologies belong to the category of combination of different Wicksell Structures,

Multiple and Reswitching of techniques follow. As there is no apriori reason to assume that techniques in general should belong to any one Wicksell Structure, the problem of choice of techniques over the development span, accompanied by changes in wage rates, gets complicated. For, in this case, the set of techniques which are eligible at a particular wage rate may not continue to be so at a different wage rate. Further, some of the techniques which were inferior at $w = w_o$ (say) may join the set of eligible techniques at $w = w_1$, while some of the techniques which were eligible at $w = w_o$ may be inferior at $w = w_1$. In other words, the composition of the set of viable techniques is volatile, in general, when techniques belonging to different Wicksell Structures, including ones which are combinations of different Wicksell Structures are considered. In this case, the possibility of a technique termed 'inferior' at a given wage rate joining the ranks of eligible techniques at a higher wage rate cannot be ruled out.

Therefore, the techniques will have to be analysed with care, their path traced out over the entire wage span under consideration before one can decide, for what ranges of wage rates, a technique is likely to be dormant and for what ranges it emerges as an active competitor or as a dominating technique. Further, it can be shown that when techniques 'switch' over the wage span under consideration, if the economy is made to switch techniques as often as the maximum wage rate/rate of profit criteria dictates, it may, not lead to maximization of the overall rate of growth. For instance, consider the following diagram which shows three techniques which switch. The techniques are $\alpha$, $\beta$ and $\gamma$. From the diagram it is clear that the path dictated by the maximum rate of profit would be AB along technique $\alpha$, BC along technique $\beta$, CD along technique $\gamma$ and DE along technique $\beta$ once again.

However, if the switches are to be operationally meaningful, it implies the structure of capital goods change with each switch. While on AB the economy uses and produces the $\alpha$ capital good only to discard the $\alpha$ goods to produce $\beta$ capital goods when the economy switches to $\beta$ technique, along BC. At C the techniques $\beta$ and $\gamma$ switch, therefore, after this switch point if the economy switches to $\gamma$, $\beta$ capital goods are

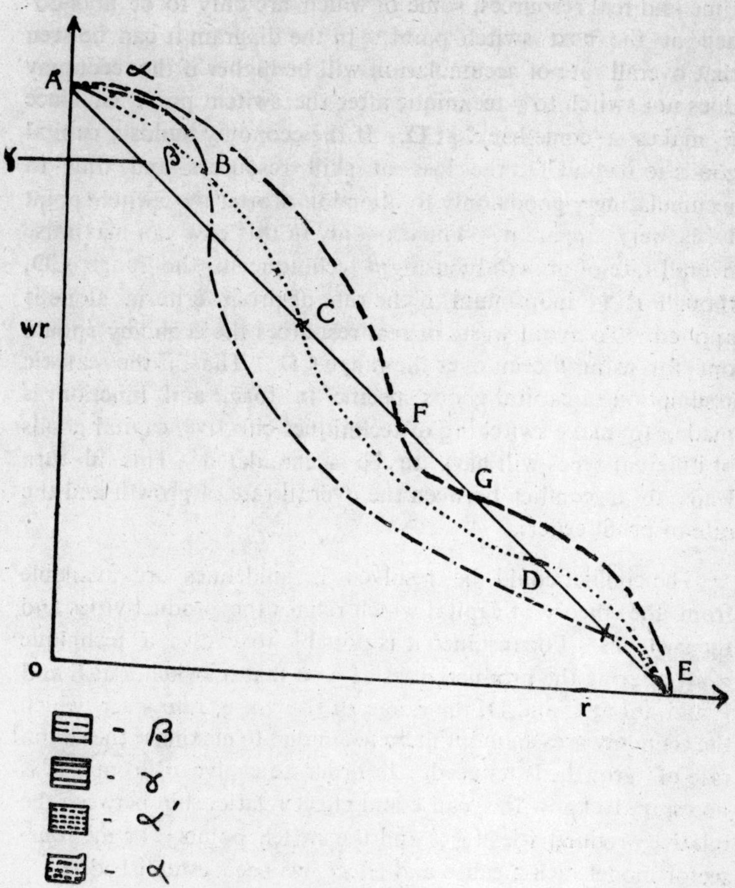


**Diagram I**

discarded and γ capital goods are produced. At the switch point D the technique β makes a 'come-back'. Thus, if the economy switches, techniques as many times as the rate of profit criteria dictates capital goods pertaining to different techniques have to be built only to be discarded at the next switch. If malleability of capital is not assumed, to make each switch operational, stocks of capital goods corresponding to different techniques will have to be built which required skill, time and real resources, some of which are only to be abondoned at the next switch point. In the diagram it can be seen that overall rate of accumulation will be higher if the economy does not switch to $\gamma$ technique after the switch point C, since $\beta$ makes a 'come-back' at D. If the economy builds $\gamma$ capital goods to be on CD, the loss of skill resources and time in accumulating $\gamma$-goods only to abondon it after the switch point D is very apparent. The economy in this case can maximise overall rate of growth by using $\beta$ technique in the range CD, though it is inoptimum if the rate of profit criteria alone is applied. To avoid waste of real resources the economy should opt for using $\beta$ even over the range CD. Thus, if the realistic assumption of capital goods specific in form and function is made, to make switching of techniques effective, capital goods of different types will have to be accumulated. This in turn leads to a conflict between the overall rate of growth and the rate of profit criteria.

The conflict could be resolved if guidelines are available from the theory of capital which relates the productivities and the switches. For instance it is possible to evolve a technique $\alpha'$ by altering the productivities of $\alpha$ so that it switches at E and F and not at C and D, the range of the wage rate over which the economy uses an inoptimum technique to maximise the overall rate of growth is reduced. In order to evolve $\alpha'$ from $\alpha$ it is necessary to know the cause and effect relationship between the relative productivities ($\triangle_s$) and the switch points. For the four-sector model such a cause and effect has been established.

Further, it is possible to suggest what specific changes are needed to be brought about in the relative productivities ($\triangle_s$) to evolve a new technique which will be an improvement in terms of its growth potential over the development path.

The analysis of the four-sector model, conducted with all its limitations, suggests that when capital theory is developed with Sraffa-Neumann model as its basis, which means self-sufficient systems of inter-dependent set of processes, with heterogeneous inputs and outputs, including capital goods it can offer guidelines to problems connected with the dynamic process of accumulation with changing capital structure. In other words, a path of development over time with changing distribution, can be worked out so as to maximise the overall rate of growth.

## REFERENCES


1. The first edition of the Accumulation of Capital was published in 1956 in which Joan Robinson discusses the 'Perverse' case in Chapter 10. Sraffa's book was published much later in 1960. In the 3rd edition of Accumulation of Capital, (1966) Joan Robinson has added a post script to the Chapter on choice of Techniques, wherein she states "It is not abnormal for the Wicksell Effect to be negative". See J. Robinson : *The Accumulation of Capital*, (Macmillan 1956) Chapter 10, and J. Robinson : *The Accumulation of Capital*, (Macmillan 1966), Chapter 10, p. 113.
2. D. G. Champernowne : 'The Production Function and the Theory of Capital : A Comment' *Review of Economic Studies*, (Vol. 21, 1953-54) pp. 112-35.
3. L. L. Pasinetti : 'Changes in the Rate of Profit and Switches of Techniques', *Quarterly Journal of Economics*, (Vol. 80, 1966), pp. 503-17.
4. M. Bruno, E. Burmeister and E. Sheshinski : "The Nature and Implications of the Reswitching of Techniques" Quarterly Journal of Economics, (Vol. 80, 1966) pp. 526-53.
5. *Op. cit.* 3.
6. P. Sraffa : *Production of Commodities by Means of Commodities*, (Cambridge University Press, 1960).
7. G. Mathur : *Planning for Steady Growth*, (Basil Blackwell, Oxford 1965), pp. 45-48.
8. *Ibid.*, pp. 159-160.
9. *Ibid.*, pp. 160-161.
10. *Ibid.*, p. 161.
11. *Ibid.*, pp. 55-62, 156 to 158.
12. *Ibid.*
13. *Ibid.*, pp. 159-161.
14. G. Mathur : 'On the Neutral Barton and Bartonesque Effects', (Section IV, 1973), Unpublished.
15. *Ibid.*

# Appendix to Chapter IV

CONSIDER THE technology A, with uniform wage rate W and Coefficient of profit R in all the processes. $P_1$, $P_2$, $P_3$ and $P_4$ are the prices of the equipments $e_1$, $e_2$, $e_3$ and $e_4$ in terms of $P_o$, the price of Corn. The wage (W) in this system is paid in advance of production in terms of Corn, the numeraire for the system of prices. The workers consume their entire wage W paid in advance of production and entrepreneurs do not consume out of their profits.

TECHNOLOGY A

| Men | C | $e_1$ | $e_2$ | $e_3$ | $e_4$ | | C | $e_1$ | $e_2$ | $e_3$ | $e_4$ |
|---|---|---|---|---|---|---|---|---|---|---|---|
| 1 | W | 1 | 0 | 0 | 0 | —— | 25 | 1 | 0 | 0 | 0 |
| 1 | W | 0 | 1 | 0 | 0 | —— | 0 | 16 | 1 | 0 | 0 |
| 1 | W | 0 | 0 | 1 | 0 | —— | 0 | 0 | 1 | 1 | 0 |
| 1 | W | 0 | 0 | 0 | 1 | —— | 0 | 0 | 0 | 14 | 1 |
| 1 | W | 0 | 0 | 0 | 1 | —— | 0 | 0 | 0 | 0 | 6 + 1 |

The equation[1] which establishes the link between w $\gamma$ (where $\gamma$ stands for the coefficient of growth) with the rate of interest i, for the technology with four sectors in the investment department is,

$$w\gamma = \frac{b_0 b_1 b_2 b_3}{b_1 b_2 b_3 b_4 - (b_2 b_3 \triangle_1 i + i^2 b_3 \triangle_2 + i^3 \triangle_3)}$$

Where $\triangle_1 = (b_1 - b_4)$, $\triangle_2 = (b_2 - b_4)$ and $\triangle_3 = (b_3 - b_4)$.

The price equations for the technology A, are,

$$(W + P_1)\, R = 25P_0 + P_1 \qquad \ldots\ldots (1)$$

$$(W + P_2)\, R = 16P_1 + P_2 \qquad \ldots\ldots (2)$$

$$(W + P_3)\, R = P_2 + P_3 \qquad \ldots\ldots (3)$$

$$(W + P_4)\, R = 14P_3 + P_4 \qquad \ldots\ldots (4)$$

$$(W + P_4)\, R = 7P_4 \qquad \ldots\ldots (5)$$

In the above set of five equations, the unknowns are the wage rate W, the coefficient of profit R and the prices $P_0$, $P_1$, $P_2$, $P_3$, and $P_4$. As the five equations are independent, it is a case of five equations and seven unknowns. The number of unknowns can be reduced to five if R or W is given and $P_0$ is taken as the numeraire. In other words the relative prices can be computed, given distribution.

However, a set of five non-linear simultaneous equations are difficult to solve unless one uses the computer. But the problem can be overcome easily if the equation,

$$w\gamma = \frac{b_0 b_1 b_2 b_3}{b_1 b_2 b_3 b_4 - [i b_2 b_3 \triangle_1 + b_3 i^2 \triangle_2 + i^3 \triangle_3]}$$

is also considered. For example, for technology A,

---

1. G. Mathur : *Planning for Steady Growth,* (Oxford University Press, 1965), pp. 55-62 and 156-158.

$$w\,\gamma = \frac{25\times16\times1\times14}{16\times1\times14\times6 - [14\times10\times i + i^2\times14\,(-5) + i^3\times8]}$$

From the above equation if $i = \gamma = 2.5$ the wage rate w can be derived for the technology A give $i = 2.5$ as follows:

$$w\,\gamma = \frac{5600}{1344 - [14\times10\times2.5 + 2.5\times2.5\,(-5)\times14 + 2.5^3\times8]}$$

$$= \frac{5600}{1344 - (350 - 437.5 + 125)} = \frac{5600}{1344 - 37.5}$$

$$w\,\gamma = \frac{5600}{1306.5} = 4.286261$$

As $\gamma = 1 + g$ where g is the rate of growth, $g = 2.5$ as $g = r$ in Sraffa Neumann Model under the assumption of $se = 1$, $sw = 0$ and workers do not get a share in the surplus.

$$\text{Therefore, } W = \frac{4.28621}{3.5} = 1.224646$$

The price equations for technology A with $W = 1.22$ and $R = 3.5$ are,

$$(1.22 + P_1)\,3.5 = 25\,P_0 + P_1 \qquad \ldots\ldots (1)$$

$$(1.22 + P_2)\,3.5 = 16\,P_1 + P_2 \qquad \ldots\ldots (2)$$

$$(1.22 + P_3)\,3.5 = P_2 + P_3 \qquad \ldots\ldots (3)$$

$$(1.22 + P_4)\,3.5 = 14\,P_3 + P_4 \qquad \ldots\ldots (4)$$

$$(1.22 + P_4)\,3.5 = 7\,P_4 \qquad \ldots\ldots (5)$$

From equation (5), $(1.22 + P_4)\,3.5 = 7\,P_4$

$$3.5\,P_4 = 4.27$$

$$P_4 = 1.22$$

Substituting the value of $P_4$ in equation (4) we get,

$$(1.22 + 1.22)\ 3.5 = 14\ P_3 + 1.22$$

$$\frac{2.44 \times 3.5 - 1.22}{14} = P_3 = 0.5228571$$

Substituting the value of $P_3$ in equation (3),

$$(1.22 + P_3)\ 3.5 = P_2 + P_3$$

$$3.5 \times 1.22 + 2.5 \times 0.523 = P_2$$

$$P_2 = 4.27 + 1.3075$$

$$P_2 = 5.5771428$$

Substituting the value of $P_2$ in equation (2),

$$(1.22 + P_2)\ 3.5 = 16\ P_1 + P_2$$

$$4.27 + 2.5 \times 5.578 = 16\ P_1$$

$$P_1 = \frac{18.215}{16}$$

$$P_1 = 1.1383036$$

Substituting the value of $P_1$ in equation (1),

$$(1.22 + P_1)\ 3.5 = 25\ P_0 + P_1\ (1)$$

$$P_0 = \frac{4.27 + 2.5 \times 1.1383}{25}$$

$$P_0 = 0.28463 \simeq 0.285$$

If $P_0$ is taken as the numeraire, the relative prices are for $\gamma = R = 3.5$ and $w = 1.22$.

| $P_0$ | : | $P_1$ | : | $P_2$ | : | $P_3$ | : | $P_4$ |
|---|---|---|---|---|---|---|---|---|
| 1 | : | 3.999 | : | 19.594 | : | 1.837 | : | 4.286 |

Similarly the relative prices for the technology A can be worked out for i = 3.094, 4.5, 5 and 6.5.

The technology A switches with Neutral Wicksell Technology with the same order of mechanization, *i.e.* with the technology $A_1$

TECHNOLOGY A

| Men | C | $E_1$ | $E_2$ | $E_3$ | $E_4$ | | C | $E_1$ | $E_2$ | $E_3$ | $E_4$ |
|---|---|---|---|---|---|---|---|---|---|---|---|
| 1 | W | 1 | 0 | 0 | 0 | —— | 5 | 1 | 0 | 0 | 0 |
| 1 | W | 0 | 1 | 0 | 0 | —— | 0 | 6 | 1 | 0 | 0 |
| 1 | W | 0 | 0 | 1 | 0 | —— | 0 | 0 | 6 | 1 | 0 |
| 1 | W | 0 | 0 | 0 | 1 | —— | 0 | 0 | 0 | 6 | 1 |
| 1 | W | 0 | 0 | 0 | 1 | —— | 0 | 0 | 0 | 0 | 6+1 |

Using the necessary condition for switching for Technology A we can find the interest (profit) rates at which it switches with $A_1$ as follows,

$$w\gamma = \frac{5600}{16 \times 14 \times 6 - (140\, i - 5 \times 14\, i^2 + i^3 \times 8)}$$

The necessary condition is,

$$8\, i^3 - 70\, i^2 + 140\, i = 0$$

$$i = 0 \text{ or, } 8\, i^2 - 70\, i + 140 = 0$$

$$i = \frac{70 \pm \sqrt{70 \times 70 - 4 \times 8 \times 140}}{2 \times 8}$$

$$= \frac{70 \pm \sqrt{4900 - 4480}}{2 \times 8}$$

$$= \frac{70 \pm \sqrt{420}}{2 \times 8} = \frac{70 \pm 20.493902}{16}$$

$$i = \frac{90.493902}{16} = 5.6558689$$

$$\text{and } i = \frac{49.506098}{16} = 3.0941311$$

Thus, the two switch points are i = 3.094 and 5.660.

# Appendix to Chapter V

## THE NECESSARY AND SUFFICIENT CONDITION FOR DOUBLE SWITCHING

IT WAS established in Chapter V, that if Double Switching is to take place the number of departments in the I-Sector must be four or more.

However as every four sector model need not lead to Double Switching, the necessary condition for Double Switching has to be analysed.

Consider a technology T, with four departments in the I-Sector, the diagonal elements of productivities per man equipment team are $b_1$, $b_2$, $b_3$ and $b_4$.

TECHNOLOGY T

| Men | C | $E_1$ | $E_2$ | $E_3$ | $E_4$ | | C | $E_1$ | $E_2$ | $E_3$ | $E_4$ |
|---|---|---|---|---|---|---|---|---|---|---|---|
| 1 | W | 1 | 0 | 0 | 0 | ——— | $b_0$ | 1 | 0 | 0 | 0 |
| 1 | W | 0 | 1 | 0 | 0 | ——— | 0 | $b_1$ | 1 | 0 | 0 |
| 1 | W | 0 | 0 | 1 | 0 | ——— | 0 | 0 | $b_2$ | 1 | 0 |
| 1 | W | 0 | 0 | 0 | 1 | ——— | 0 | 0 | 0 | $b_3$ | 1 |
| 1 | W | 0 | 0 | 0 | 1 | ——— | 0 | 0 | 0 | 0 | $b_4+1$ |

If $\triangle_1 = b_1 - b_4$ and $\triangle_2 = b_2 - b_4$ $\triangle_3 = b_3 - b_4$, then the equation connecting $w\gamma$ with i through productivities is given by,

$$w\gamma = \frac{b_0 b_1 b_2 b_3}{b_1 b_2 b_3 b_4 - (b_2 b_3 \triangle_1 i + b_3 \triangle_2 i^2 + i^3 \triangle_3)}$$

If $\phi(i) = i(b_2 b_3 \triangle_1 + b_3 \triangle_2 i + i^2 \triangle_3)$,

the $(w\gamma - i)$ equation becomes linear if $\phi(i) = 0$. This implies that for some value or values of i, the technology T switches with a Neutral Wicksell Technology of the same order of mechanization. At a switch point, therefore $\phi(i) = 0$.

When $\phi(i) = 0$ either $i = 0$ or

$$b_2 b_3 \triangle_1 + i b_3 \triangle_2 + i^2 \triangle_3 = 0$$

or the determinant

$$D = \begin{vmatrix} \triangle_1 & -\triangle_2 & \triangle_2 \\ i & b_2 & 0 \\ 0 & i & b_3 \end{vmatrix} = 0$$

Thus for Double switching it is necessary that the equation $D = 0$ must have two real and positive roots. Therefore, consider the solution,

$$i = \frac{-b_3 \triangle_2 + \sqrt{b_3^2 \triangle_2^2 - 4\triangle_3 \triangle_1 b_2 b_3}}{2\triangle_3}$$

I(a) When $\triangle_2 > 0$, then if $b_3 \Delta_2 > \sqrt{A}$, the numerator is negative, therefore, $\triangle_3$ must be negative for i to be positive. If $\triangle_2 > 0$, $\triangle_3 < 0$ also $\triangle_2 b_3 > \sqrt{A}$, it means $\triangle_1$ is negative for i to be positive.

Therefore for i to be positive,

$$\Delta_2 > 0, \Delta_1 < 0, \Delta_3 < 0 \qquad \text{......(1)}$$

I(b) If $\Delta_2 > 0$, if $\Delta_2 b_3 < \sqrt{A}$, the numerator is positive, therefore $\Delta_3 > 0$. Also $\Delta_2 b_3 < \sqrt{A}$ means $\Delta_1$ must be negative for i to be positive,

*i.e.* $\Delta_2 > 0, \Delta_1 < 0, \Delta_3 < 0$ ......(2)

I(c) If $\Delta_2 < 0$, and $\Delta_2 b_3 < \sqrt{A}$ in this case the numerator is positive, therefore $\Delta_3 > 0$ for i to be positive, ......(3)

II(a) If $\Delta_2 > 0$, $\Delta_2 b_3 < \sqrt{A}$, the numerator is negative, therefore $\Delta_3 < 0$, also $\Delta_1 < 0$ for i to be positive, ......(4)

II(b) If $\Delta_2 < 0$, $\Delta_2 b_3 > \sqrt{A}$, the numerator is positive therefore, $\Delta_3 > 0$ also $\Delta_1 > 0$ for i to be positive,
*i.e.* $\Delta_1 > 0, \Delta_2 < 0, \Delta_3 > 0$ ......(5)

II(c) If $\Delta_2 < 0$ and $\Delta_3 b_3 < \sqrt{A}$, the numerator is negative, therefore, $\Delta_3 < 0$ also $\Delta_1 < 0$ for i to be positive,
*i.e.* $\Delta_1 < 0, \Delta_2 < 0, \Delta_3 < 0$ ......(6)

As (1) and (4) are compatible for the same technique, two positive real roots are possible if in a technique the productivities are such as to have $\Delta_1 < 0$, $\Delta_2 > 0$, $\Delta_3 < 0$, Also, (3) and (5) are compatible for the same technology. Therefore, two positive real roots are possible if $\Delta_1 > 0$, $\Delta_2 < 0$, $\Delta_3 > 0$. Therefore, the necessary condition for two positive and real roots (double switching) is $\Delta_2$ and $\Delta_1$, $\Delta_3$ must have opposite signs.

The technology must, therefore, be either of type A or B.

| A | | | B | | |
|---|---|---|---|---|---|
| $b_0$ | = | $b_0$ | $b_0$ | = | $b_0$ |
| $b_1$ | < | $b_4$ | $b_1$ | > | $b_4$ |
| $b_2$ | > | $b_4$ | $b_2$ | < | $b_4$ |
| $b_3$ | < | $b_4$ | $b_3$ | > | $b_4$ |
| $b_4$ | = | $b_4$ | $b_4$ | = | $b_4$ |

However, a combination of Wicksell structure like A or B technologies is only a necessary condition for double switching, for every combination technique may not double switch within the relevant range of the rates of interest (or wage rates).

The sufficient condition is that the equation D = 0 must have roots between 0 and $b_4$.

# Bibliography

## Books


Allen, R.G.D., *Mathematical Analysis for Economists*, (London, Macmillan), 1938.

Baumol, W.J., *Economic Dynamics : An Introduction*, (Macmillan) 1963.

Blatt, J.M., *Dynamic Economic Systems—A Post Keynesian Approach*, (Great Britain : Wheatsheaf Books), 1983.

Blaug, M., *Economic Theory in Retrospect*, (London, Hannemann, 2nd ed.), 1968.

Bohm-Bawerk, *The Positive Theory of Capital*, (W.A. Smart's Translation) 1891.

Clark, J.B., *The Distribution of Wealth*, (Macmillan), 1927.

Dobb, M.H., *An Essay on Economic Growth and Planning*, (London, Routledge and Kegan Paul), 1960.

*Theories of value and Distribution since Adam Smith*, (C.U.P.—Vikas Students' Edition) 1979.

Domar, E.D., *Essays in the Theory of Growth* (London : Oxford University Press) 1957.

Dosso, *Linear Programming and Economic Analysis*, (New York, McGraw Hill) 1958.

Ekelund Jr. R.B., and R.F. Hebert, *A History of Economic Theory and Method*, (McGraw Hill, International Student Edition) 1983.

Ferguson, C.E., *The Neo-Classical Theory of Production and Distribution*, (Cambridge : Cambridge University Press), 1969.

Fisher, Irving, *The Theory of Interest* (New York : Macmillan) 1930.

Gerschenkron, A., "Economic Backwardness in Historical Perspective" in Hoselitz B. (Ed.) : *The Progress of Under-developed Areas* (Chicago) 1952.

Hahn, F.E. (Ed.), *Readings in the Theory of Growth* (London, Macmillan) 1971.

Harcourt, G.C. and Laing, N.F. (eds.), *Capital and Growth Selected Readings*, (London, Penguin Books) 1971.

Harcourt, G.C., *Some Cambridge Controversies in the Theory of Capital*, (Cambridge : Cambridge University Press), 1972.

Harcourt, G.C., Karmel, P.H. and Wallace, R.H., *Economic Activity* (Cambridge : Cambridge University Press) 1967.

Harrod, R.F., *Towards a Dynamic Economics : Some Recent Developments of Economic Theory and Their Application to Policy*, (London, Macmillan) 1948.

Hicks, J.R., *Capital and Growth*, (Oxford : Clarendon Press) 1965.

Higgins, B., *Economic Development*, (New York), 1958.

Hirschman, A.O., *The Strategy of Economic Development*, (New Haven), 1958.

Howard, M.C., *Modern Theories of Income Distribution*, (Macmillan), 1979.

Hunt, E.K. and G. Schwatz, *A Critique of Economic Theory*, (Great Britain Penguin Books) 1972.

Jevons, W.S., *The Theory of Political Economy*, (London : Macmillan), 1911.

Jones, H.G., *An Introduction to Modern Theories of Economic Growth*, (McGraw Hill) 1976.

Kaldor, N., *Essays on Value and Distribution*, (London : Duckworth) 1960.

Kalecki, M., *Essays on the Theory of Economic Fluctuations* (London : Allen and Unwin), 1939.

*Kalechi*, M., *Theory of Economic Dynamics*, (Allen and Unwin), 1964.

Keynes, J.M., *The Genernl Theory of Employment, Interest and Money*, (London : Macmillan) 1936.

Klein, L.R., *Introduction to Econometrics*, (New Delhi Prentice-Hall of India Ltd.) 1965.

Koopmans, T.C. (ed.), *Activity Analysis of Production and Allocation*, (New York, Wiley) 1951.

Kregal, J.A., *Rate of Profit, Distribution and Growth—Two Views* (Macmillan Press Ltd.) 1971.

Kregal, J.A., *The Theory of Capital*, (Macmillan) 1976.

Kuznets, S., *Six Lectures on Economic Growth* (New York : Glencoe), 1959.

Leibenstein, H., *Economic Backwardness and Economic Growth* (New York), 1957.

Leontief, W.W., *The Structure of the American Economy 1919-1939*, (2nd ed. 1951).

Lewis, W.A., *Economic Development with Unlimited Supplies of Labour*, (Manchester School), 1954.

Lutz, F.A. and Hague, D.C. (eds.), *The Theory of Capital* (London : Macmillan), 1961.

Marshall, A., *Principles of Economics* (London : Macmillan) 1966.

Marx, K., *Capital*, Vol. I (Progress Publishers), 1958.

Marx, K., *Capital*, Vol. III (Progress Publishers), 1958.

Mathur, Gautam, *Planning for Steady Growth*, (Oxford Basil Blackwell), 1965.

Meade, J.E., *A Neo-Classical Theory of Economic Growth* (London : Allen and Unwin), 1961.

Morishima, M., *Equilibrium, Stability and Growth—A Multi-Sectoral Analysis*, (Oxford : Clarendon Press) 1964.

Myrdal, G., *Economic Theory and Underdeveloped Regions*, (London), 1957.

Myrdal, Gunnar, *Objectivity in Social Research*, (London : Duckworth), 1970.

Nurkse, R., *Problems of Capital Formation in Underdeveloped* Countries, (Oxford) 1953.

Pasinetti, L.L., *Growth and Income Distribution*, (Cambridge : Cambridge University Press), 1974.

Pasinetti, L.L., *Lectures on the Theory of Production*, (Macmillan), 1978.

Pasinetti, L.L., (ed.), *Essays on the Theory of Joint Production* (Macmillan : London), 1980.

Robinson, Joan, *Introduction to the Theory of Employment*, (London : Macmillan), 1937.

Robinson, Joan, *The Accumulation of Capital*, (London ; Macmillan), 1956.

Robinson, Joan, *Essays in Economic Analysis*, (London : Macmillan), 1960.

Robinson, Joan, *Essays in the Theory of Economic Growth* (London : Macmillan), 1962.

Robinson, Joan, *Collected Economic Papers*, Vols. I, II and III (Oxford : Basal Blackwell), 1965.

Robinson, Joan, *An Essay on Marxian Economics* (Macmillan) 1966.

Robinson, Joan, *Economic Philosophy*, (Penguin Books), 1968.

Robinson, Joan, *Economic Heresies : Some Old Fashioned Questions in Economic Theory*, (New York, Basic Books), 1971.

Robinson, J. and Eatwell, J., *An Introduction to Modern Economics*, (Tata-McGraw Hill), 1974.

Salter, W.E.G., *Productivity and Technical Change*, (Cambridge : Harward University Press), 1960.

Samuelson, Paul, A., *Foundations of Economic Analysis*, (Cambridge : Harward University Press), 1947.

Sen, A.K., *Choice of Techniques : An Aspect of the Theory of Planned Economic Development*, (Oxford University Press 1972).

Sen, A.K. (ed.), *Growth Economics*, (Penguin Books), Selected Readings, 1970.

Smith, Adam, *An Inquiry into the Nature and Causes of the Wealth of Nations*, Ed. E. Cannan, (London : Methuen), 1904.

Sraffa, Piero (ed.), With the Collaboration of Dobb, M.H., *The Works and Correspondence of David Ricardo*, 10 vols. (Cambridge : Cambridge University Press), 1950-55.

Sraffa, Piero, *Production of Commodities by Means of Commodities—Prelude to a Critique of Economic Theory.* (Cambridge : Cambridge University Press), 1960.

Stigler, George, J., *Production and Distribution Theories : The Formative Period*, (New York : Macmillan), 1949.

Sweezy, P.M., *The Theory of Capitalist Development*, (Oxford University Press), 1942.

The Economics of Imperfect Competition, (London : Macmillan 2nd ed.), 1969.

Walras, L., *Elements of Pure Economics*, (London : George Allen and Unwin), 1965.

Wicksell, Knut, *Lectures on Political Economy*, Vol. 1, (London : Routledge), 1934.

# Articles

Arrow, K.J., "The Economic Implications of Learning by Doing", *Review of Economic Studies*, XXIX, 1962, pp. 152-73.

Bardhan, P.K., "An Estimation of Production Functions from International Cross Section Data", *Economic Journal* LXXVII, 1967, pp. 328-37.

Bhaduri, A., "The Concept of the Marginal Productivity of Capital and the Wicksell Effect", *Oxford Economic Papers*, XVIII, 1966, pp. 284-88.

Bhaduri, A., "On the Significance of Recent Controversies on Capital Theory : A Marxian View", *Economic Journal*, LXXIX, 1969, pp. 532-39.

Bharadwaj, K.R., "Value Through Exogeneous Distribution", *Economic Weekly*, XV, pp. 1450-54.

Bliss, C.J., "On Putty-Clay", *Review of Economic Studies* XXXV, 1968, pp. 105-32.

Bruno, M., Burmeister, E., and Sheshinski, E., "Nature and Implications of the Reswitching of Techniques", *Quarterly Journal of Economics*, LXXX, 1966, pp. 526-53.

Champernowne, D.G., "A Note of J.V. Neumann's Article on A Model of Economic Equilibrium", *Review of Economic Studies*, XIII 1945-46, pp. 10-18.

Champernowne, D.G., "The Production Function and the Theory of Capital : A Comment", *Review of Economic Studies*, XXI, 1953-54, pp. 112-35.

Chang, P., "Rate of Profit and Income Distribution in Relation to the Rate of Growth : A Comment", 1964, *Review of Economic Studies*, XXXI, pp. 103-05.

Eckstein, O., "Investment Criteria for Economic Development and the Theory of Inter-temporal Welfare Economics", *Quarterly Journal of Economics*, February 1957, No. 71, pp. 56-85.

Garegnani, P., "Switching of Techniques", *Quarterly Journal of Economics*, LXXX 1966, pp. 554-67.

Garegnani, P., "Heterogeneous Capital, the Production Function and the Theory of Distribution", *Review of Economic Studies*, 1970, XXXVII, pp. 407-36.

Harrod, R.B., "An Essay in Dynamic Theory", *Economic Journal*, 1939, XLIX, pp. 14-33.

Harcourt, G.C., "Some Cambridge Controversies in the Theory of Capital", *Journal of Economic Literature*, 1969, Vol. VII pp. 369-405.

Kaldor, N., "A Model of Economic Growth", *Economic Journal*, Vol. LXVII, December 1957.

Kaldor, N., "Alternative Theories of Distribution", *Review of Economic Studies*, Vol. XXIII, 1956.

Kaldor, N., and Mirrlees, J A., "A New Model of Economic Growth", *Review of Economic Studies*, Vol. XXIX, June 1962.

Levhari, D., "A Non-Substitution Theorem and Switching of Techniques", *Quarterly Journal of Economics*, LXXIX, pp. 98-105.

Levhari, D. and Samuelson, P.A., "The Non-Switching Theorem is False", *Quarterly Journal of Economics*, 1966, LXXX, pp. 518-19.

Little, "Classical Growth" in *Oxford Economic Papers* 1957, pp. 152-177.

Mathur, G., "On the Neutral Barton and Bartonesque Effect", (Unpublished), 1973.

Morishima, M., "Refutation of the Non-Switching Theorem", *Quarterly Journal of Economics*, 1966, LXXX, pp. 520-25.

Neumann, J.V., "A Model of General Economic Equilibrium", *Review of Economic Studies*, 1945-46, XIII, pp. 1-9.

Pasinetti, L.L., "Rate of Profit and Income Distribution in Relation to the Rate of Economic Growth", *Review of Economic Studies*, 1962, XXIX, pp. 267-79.

Pasinetti, L.L., "Changes in the Rate of Profit and Switches of Techniques", *Quarterly Journal of Economics*, LXXX, 1966, pp. 503-17.

Pasinetti, L.L., "Switches of Technique and the 'Rate of Return' in Capital Theory", *Economic Journal*, 1969, LXXIX, pp. 508-31.

Phelps, E.S., "The Golden Rule of Accumulation : A Fable for Growth-men", *American Economic Review*, Vol. LI, Sept. 1961.

Robinson, Joan, "Accumulation and the Production Function", *Economic Journal*, 1959, pp. 433-42.

Robinson, Joan, "The Production Function and the Theory of Capital", *Review of Economic Studies*, 1953-54, XXI pp. 81-106.

Robinson, Joan, "The Real Wicksell Effect", *Economic Journal*, 1958, LXVIII, pp. 600-05.

Robinson, Joan, "Equilibrium Growth Models", *American Economic Review*, 1961, LI, pp. 360-69.

Robinson, Joan, "Solow on the Rate of Return", *Economic Journal*, 1961, LXXIV, pp. 410-17.

Robinson, Joan, "The Labour Theory of Value", *Sci. Soc.* 1954, Vol. 18, pp. 141-51.

Robinson, Joan, "Piero Sraffa and the Rate of Exploitation", *New left Rev.* 1965, Vol. 31, pp. 28-34.

Robinson, Joan, "The Theory of Value Reconsidered", *Australian Economic Papers*, Vol. 8, 1968, pp. 13-19.

Robinson, Joan and Naqvi, K.A., "The Badly-Behaved Production Function", *Quarterly Journal of Economics*, 1967, LXXXI, pp. 579-91.

Rostow, W.W., "The Take-off into Self-Sustained Growth", *Economic Journal*, March 1956, No. 66, pp. 25-48.

Samuelson, P.A., "Parable and Realism in Capital Theory : The Surrogate Production Function", *Review of Economic Studies*, XXIX, 1962, pp. 193-206.

Samuelson, P.A., "A Summing Up", *Quarterly Journal of Economics*, LXXX, 1966, pp. 568-83.

Solow, "The Production Function and the Theory of Capital", *The Review of Economic Studies*, 1955-56, pp. 101-08.

Symposium : "Paradoxes in Capital Theory", *Quarterly Journal of Economics*, Vol. 80, 1966.